# PRAISE FOR *Cinderella* RULE

*The Cinderella Rule* is an excellent resource for both teenaged girls and the parents, relatives, teachers, mentors and friends who want them to seek a "prince" who will woo and pursue them. Bethany Jett's writing style is practical, full of wisdom and engaging. I plan on buying this book for my 19-year-old daughter . . . and for her boyfriend, too.

## Arron Chambers
Pastor and Author of *Remember Who You Are* and *Eats with Sinners*

In a world where young women are inundated with messages telling them to chase after the bad boy, beast or vampire, it is refreshing to hear one telling them that they are worthy of a godly prince. As a father of a teenaged girl, I appreciate Bethany's insights and advice. Both are timely and inspiring for young Cinderellas navigating the sometimes confusing world of love and dating. I laughed, I cried, I got a pedicure.

## Terry Davis
Family Minister at Journey Christian Church
Greeley, Colorado

Any girl who quotes a minion from *Despicable Me* (whaaa?) had me at hello. Bethany's charm, mixed with pop culture and a large amount of the Bible, will help the single woman who wishes to become a godly (datable) woman. *The Cinderella Rule* is a helpful guide for all the single ladies.

## Renee Fisher
Spirited Speaker and Author of *Faithbook of Jesus, Not Another Dating Book* and *Forgiving Others, Forgiving Me* (www.devotionaldiva.com)

*The Cinderella Rule* is a beautiful and compelling look at what it means to be a daughter of the King and bride of Christ. Bethany Jett does a marvelous job of pointing young women to their true beauty and value within and guides them on a journey filled with hope and promise.

Nicole O'Dell
Founder of Choose NOW Ministries
Author of *The Diamond Estates* Series

Reading *The Cinderella Rule* is like chatting with your older, cooler cousin—you know, the one who you always wanted to paint your nails and do your hair for you. Although Bethany does discuss highlights and French "manis," she also talks about something much more important and enduring—your future husband. *The Cinderella Rule* explains that Mr. Right is someone who recognizes and seeks your inner beauty and helps you shine brighter. Bethany gives a straightforward, modern, conversational how-to for loving yourself in order to find Prince Charming and live happily ever after.

Laura L. Smith
Author of *Skinny, Hot, Angry* and the *Status Updates* Series

# THE Cinderella RULE

Bethany Jett

A YOUNG WOMAN'S
GUIDE TO
Happily Ever After

**Regal**

For more information and
special offers from Regal Books, email us at
subscribe@regalbooks.com

Published by Regal
From Gospel Light
Ventura, California, U.S.A.
*www.regalbooks.com*
Printed in the U.S.A.

Published in association with the literary agency of
Amanda Luedeke of MacGregor Literary, Inc. of Hillsboro, Oregon.

Some names have been changed for confidentiality purposes.

Library of Congress Cataloging-in-Publication Data
Jett, Bethany.
The Cinderella rule : a young woman's guide to happily ever after / Bethany Jett.
pages cm
Includes bibliographical references and index.
ISBN 978-0-8307-6616-1 (trade paper : alk. paper)
1. Christian women—Conduct of life. 2. Single people—Conduct of life. 3. Dating
(Social customs)—Religious aspects—Christianity. I. Title.
BJ1610.J48 2013
248.8'43—dc23
2013003181

Rights for publishing this book outside the U.S.A. or in non-English languages are
administered by Gospel Light Worldwide, an international not-for-profit ministry.
For additional information, please visit www.glww.org, email info@glww.org, or write to
Gospel Light Worldwide, 1957 Eastman Avenue, Ventura, CA 93003, U.S.A.

To order copies of this book and other Regal products in bulk quantities,
please contact us at 1-800-446-7735.

For Tara, Siobhan, and Natalie

*"It is a truth universally acknowledged, that a single man in possession of a good fortune must be in want of a wife."*
JANE AUSTEN, PRIDE AND PREJUDICE

*My girls, you are the fortune.*
*I'm so proud of the women you've become,*
*and I love you from the bottom of my heart.*

# Contents

# Acknowledgments

To God be the glory. Let my words be worthy (see Jer. 15:19).

Justin Jett, the man of my dreams: It was always you. 05=45. You are an amazing husband and father. Your unwavering belief in me gave me the confidence to pursue my heart's desires. Thank you for stepping into every role needed while we pursued this dream. I owe you a million loads of laundry.

Jeremiah, Jedidiah, and Josiah: Thanks for being so good for Daddy while Mommy was writing. You three are the delight of my life. I love you millions and millions and more. My prayer is that you are Prince Charmings for the girls who allow you to pursue them.

My mom, Johnnie Alexander Donley: for tirelessly reading, editing and critiquing. I owe my love of words to you. I'm glad you know how much I adore you.

My dad, Jeffery R. W. Donley: Thank you for teaching me the absoluteness of God's truth. I appreciate your prayers, encouragement and support. Don't paint with a shovel. I love you.

Jill and Nathaniel: I've always tried to be the best role model possible, and I hope nothing you read embarrasses you or makes you think less of me. I'm so proud of who you have both become. You're the best siblings in the entire world. I love you always. Spirish forever.

My agent, Amanda Luedeke: God directed our paths to the lounge sitting area that last night of the conference. Bella Jacket! Thanks for seeing potential. You are amazing, and I am so thankful to have you in my life. I'm excited about our journey!

Steve Lawson: Your *no* made your *yes* that much sweeter. Thanks for believing in the story. You're my champion.

Kim, Jackie, Mark, Julia, Rob and everyone at Regal Publishing: Your kindness, expertise and openness made this overwhelming process easier on a newbie. Thanks for all the hard work and dedication you've put into not only this book, but me. You guys are fantastic!

Cecil Murphey: Your generosity in bestowing the scholarships for the FCWC was how God opened the door for this journey. I am forever grateful.

Clella Camp, the best roommate I've ever had: Thank you for your wisdom and guidance. I wouldn't have gone to the conference if it hadn't been for you.

To the Kindred Heart Writers: I love you all. Thanks for adopting me as a junior member.

To my Dream Team: Thank you for taking the time to give me your opinion. I love you.

To my friends: Thank you for your prayers, encouragement and patience.

# Introduction

Cinderella got it right.

Ariel chased Eric, Belle saved the Beast and, while both Princess Aurora and Snow White slept, Prince Charming pursued his lady. He knew what he wanted; and what he wanted was mild, modest, mysterious Cinderella. Though unknowingly, she let herself be pursued.

Being pursued is fun.

I remember daydreaming about when I'd meet my future husband. Would he be cute? Tall? Funny? Would it be love at first sight, or was he someone I already knew? The fantasy of meeting him became an obsession. Every guy who crossed my path caused the daydreamer voice in my mind to shout, "This could be him!" "What if he's the one?"

Was he the guy behind the counter at Subway?

Or maybe the cute waiter who winked at me?

The pizza delivery guy?

Why didn't my fantasies include rich men in fancy cars? Why was there usually food involved?

I dreamt of our story, eager to experience it. I prayed that we'd meet early in life. "God, please bring him to me soon. We don't have to get married right away—I just want time to hang out."

Thankfully, God didn't make me wait long. I was 19 when Justin walked into my receptionist office at Florida Christian College. It was attraction at first sight. He made me so nervous that I grabbed a stack of mail and turned away from him to sort it. I shot a sneak peek over my shoulder to see if he was watching me.

Justin says that's the moment he knew he had me.

While Justin thinks he "had me," I knew better. Being pursued, while easy, is purposeful. Intentional. Deliberate. It's not just about getting a guy's attention—it's a process of ensuring that he's *the one*. Of all the men holding glass slippers, he has to be your perfect fit.

How do you become purposeful and intentional about being pursued by the right one? Start praying for your man now. Pray for him to remain pure. Pray for him to have strength. Pray for his safety. Likewise, pray for God to reveal where you need to grow. The more awesome you are, the more amazing the guy is that God has waiting for you. Isn't that fantastic?!

I know the wait might be long. I've watched friends suffer through agonizing years of waiting; but when they found their mate, they all said they would have waited even longer to end up together.

The Bible tells a story in Genesis of a man who loved a woman so much that he worked for her father for 14 years so that he could marry her. The years seemed like only a few days because of Jacob's love for Rachel (see Gen. 29:20). It's the ultimate story of pursuit, and it's a testament to how men operate. A man who works hard to get his woman is extremely unlikely to cheat on her. She is valuable to him because he had to work hard to get her *and keep her*.

The more time, resources and money we invest in something (or someone), the tighter we hold onto it. For example, if you work hard to save for your first car, you're more likely to take care of that car than if your parents could easily replace it. Why? Because your time, energy and, perhaps sweat (eww!), went into your investment.

I want to be crystal clear on what you can expect from this book. There is no condemnation, no judgment, no criticism. Every word has been written with care, love and respect. There may be times when you don't like what I say, and that's okay. I'm sharing the best way to end up with a lasting, happily-ever-after romance.

Justin's and my journey to each other wasn't always an easy one, and no two paths are exactly the same. However, high standards and strong principles make your chances of ending up with Mr. Wonderful more than just wishful thinking or a fleeting fancy—which means you may have to adapt to some new concepts and change your way of thinking. "If you keep doing what you're doing, you'll keep getting what you've been getting"; and if things aren't going well, maybe there are some areas you need to tweak.[1]

If it hurts, squeeze my hand; I'm with you the whole way.

Because I look to the Bible as my source of ultimate wisdom, I quote it often. After all, who is more qualified to tell you how to end up with the love of your life than the One who created love in the first place?

When you allow yourself to be pursued, you give the guy the opportunity to invest in you while you determine how much of yourself to share. It's okay to let a guy work to get you—God created men with a great desire to work. In fact, He gave Adam a job naming the animals to keep him out of trouble (see Gen. 2:15-20).

A man can't chase you if you aren't running—and girlfriend, that's what I am going to teach you to do. We're not going to sprint; we're only gonna jog a few steps ahead.

Every race has a prize, and in this race, the prize is your heart. We're talking about the first place, gold medal, blue ribbon kind of prize, not the participant's ribbon everyone gets for showing up. Our hearts are to be protected. As the Bible says, "Above all else, guard your heart, for it is the wellspring of life" (Prov. 4:23).

Just like runners train for their race, we must train for ours. When my husband prepared for a marathon race, he cut soda from his diet and drank more water. He ate less ice cream and snacked on fruit. In the same way, when you're waiting to meet your man, you need to focus on becoming a woman worth pursuing. (Eating more fruit couldn't hurt either.)

Honestly, chasing a guy is exhausting. Most guys will do *anything* with *anyone,* and high school and college guys, in particular, are not known for their exclusivity. Raging hormones dictate many a guy's decisions; and if you pursue him, you won't ever be sure whether it's his heart or his hormones that loves you more.

When a guy sees a girl he wants, he goes after her. Similar to a lion stalking his prey, a man will overcome any obstacle to get the woman he wants. I'm not talking about creepy stalker behavior. I'm talking about romantic, I-can't-get-her-out-of-my-head intensity. When a worthy guy desires you like that, girl, watch out!

But you'll be ready.

You'll know how to look.

How to dress.

How to act.

Ladies, the strategy is simple: Justin chased; I dated him. He stopped pursuing; I broke up with him. He chased again; I took him back. He pursued while we were dating; I married him.

When the right man starts the pursuit, let him.

I'm gonna show you how.

**Note**

1. J. Herrington, M. Bonem and J. Furr, *Leading Congregational Change* (New York: Jossey-Bass, 2000).

# 1

# *Confidence*

*It is difficult to make a man miserable while he feels worthy of himself
and claims kindred to the great God who made him.*

ABRAHAM LINCOLN

Confidence is sexy.

Yet, confidence with no foundation of character or personality is hollow and vain. Like a large chocolate Easter bunny, it promises an abundance of goodness, but the first bite confirms there's more air than substance.

## Self-Esteem or God-Esteem?

Curiously, the Bible never tells us to be confident in ourselves. I've looked for passages on self-esteem, and for the most part, they are nonexistent. Instead, I found things like, "The one who calls you is faithful and he will do it" (1 Thess. 5:24), or "I can do everything through him who gives me strength" (Phil. 4:13). And how about this? "Trust in the LORD with all your heart and lean not on your own understanding" (Prov. 3:5).

I've never forgotten what my youth minister, Mark, said when he preached on self-esteem. He said, "Self-esteem doesn't exist. Self-esteem should be called 'God-esteem' because how you feel about yourself ultimately depicts how you feel toward God. We have to take ourselves out of the equation."

It took a while for me to incorporate that idea into the way I viewed myself. My confidence level had always been based on the view through others' eyes. In high school, I found confidence in cheerleading and in being Mark's "number one" kid in youth group. I had a wake-up call in college—the kids in my honors classes were the smartest kids I'd ever been around. I wasn't at the top of the class anymore. I was no longer the teacher's pet.

I'd placed my worth in the measure of my intelligence for so long that my world crumpled when the coursework required hours of study and the lessons were no longer easy. My personal demons of loneliness set up camp in every area of my life. Instead of making new friends, I retreated into myself.

If you find yourself doing this, please talk to someone and get a bigger perspective. Maybe I was also experiencing a mild form of depression, which is surely more common among young people than we give credence. When you feel like you have no one, pray for God to bring someone—specifically a girlfriend. As girls, we crave that masculine counterpart, but we have to be satisfied with ourselves before we can be truly effective for others.

## Appearance

There's a thin line separating confidence from conceit. "It's amazing how one person can be overly confident and totally insecure at the same time," my sister informed me, after earlier that morning I'd treated her like my assistant by handing her my bag, walking in front of her and then turning my head as if to say, "Ta-ta, hurry up." Yet just an hour before, I was freaking out because my hair wasn't cooperating, and I was trying to look cute for the event we were attending.

She was right, though it wasn't so much that I wanted other people to think I was pretty, as much as *I* wanted to think I'm pretty. Because, if I'm honest, on my "pretty days" I move mountains. Confidence overfloweth, and I'm able to achieve and accomplish more than on days when I feel ugly.

While I admit to temporary periods of vanity, I can't live there. The root of narcissism is insecurity, so I feel like it's a daily war I fight with myself. I know that true beauty comes from within and God looks at the heart (see 1 Sam. 16:7), but I want to be pretty because being attractive flings open doors that unattractive people have to push through. Not only do you receive better service and make first-rate impressions, but people want to be around you when they appreciate your appearance.

Think of Julia Roberts in the film *Pretty Woman*. She gets shunned by the saleswoman at a high-end department store when she wears her prostitute clothing—even though she is carrying Richard Gere's no-limit credit card. After hearing how she was snubbed, he takes her on a shopping spree and she returns to the first store wearing designer labels.

Naturally, the saleswoman doesn't recognize her. Roberts holds up her many shopping bags and asks, "You work on commission, right?" The saleswoman, confused, nods her head. Then Roberts delivers her classic line as she shakes the bags at the woman: "Big mistake. Big. Huge." If the saleswoman hadn't been such a snob, she would have made a lot of money off of Julia's purchases. We miss out when we judge people.

Makeup, a current hairstyle and fashionable, well-fitted clothing are essential components that help give confidence to those of us afraid to go out in public barefaced and looking frumpy.

Before I leave the house, I take a looooong look in the mirror. Where are my weak spots? Is the view from behind acceptable? Are my jeans hitting an inch above the floor? Have I used eye-catching accessories to draw attention away from my problem areas? Is my hair in need of a freshening spray of dry shampoo? Have I checked my nose and teeth for any embarrassing stowaways?

Why the self-interrogation?

Most women are body language experts.

We can sense a person's feelings, mood and temperament before we've been introduced. We can look at another girl and pick out five of her insecurities in no time flat. Is she nervously clutching anything? Is she hiding chipped fingernails? Does she show

her teeth when she smiles? Is her outfit put together, or is she trying to hide her body with loose-fitting clothing? Does she sit with
a bag, purse or sofa cushion hiding her stomach? Where is she
overcompensating? Am I prettier than her? Is she prettier than me?

In college, I realized an unspoken girl rule: "Intimidate or be
intimidated."

I felt intimidated by a beautiful blonde girl the first day of my
college French class. I'd scouted out the female competition before she arrived and ranked myself in the top three. Once she
walked in, she knocked us all out. And she knew it. Every male eye
watched her walk to a seat her friend had saved for her. My shoulders slumped as I physically deflated and felt like the ugly duckling
next to the grandiose swan. She was intimidating, and I wanted
the same attention she received.

····································································

Real confidence isn't grounded in our appearance.

····································································

Since I won't be seen without at least having put on powder
and mascara, I still have a few issues! However, real confidence
isn't grounded in our appearance. The Bible says that Jesus wasn't
handsome to look at—that nothing in His appearance would make
us desire Him (see Isa. 53:2). His charismatic, compassionate,
beautiful personality drew crowds to Him. Then don't you think
our focus should be on our character? Cosmetics are just icing on
the cake. I wish I could tattoo that truth on my brain.

## Talents and Dreams

Building confidence begins at such an early age.

What do you remember wanting to be when you were a little
girl? Are you taking steps toward that dream? (My brother wanted
to be Chuck E. Cheese, so naturally some dreams need to be left at
the wayside.) Are any of your dreams stranded? Left alone to die a
slow death outside in the cold rain?

My goal was not to be perfect, but for every[one?]. It wasn't enough to please my parents or God. I [fan]tasized that people whispered about how g[reat?] walked by. "There goes the smart girl." "That g[irl has the best?] SAT scores in her whole school." "She's destined for big things."

How in the world could I know what people were thinking? As if I was so important that anyone thought anything when I walked by. I had a major issue with self-importance, even if it was in my own mind. I'd created this imaginary world where I was the star and the world around was my stage. Yet you'd never have known that just by looking at the mousy, long-haired brunette.

For all those quiet dreamers out there, I'm with ya. I promise, you can do great things. You don't have to be flashy, loud or be a troublemaker. Get good grades, obey your parents, and be a listening ear to those who need you. The rewards for that kind of behavior are priceless: pride in your work, the respect of adults and peers, and few regrets.

But for you to stay balanced, you have to live a little. One of the reasons Justin is great for me is because he coaxes the sense of adventure I've squashed. Interestingly, the only times I get in "trouble" are with him (like when I got pulled over for his expired license tag, since he hadn't attached the renewed decal). Even so, I need him. He makes me forget about trying to be Miss Goody-Two-Shoes. It's okay if I'm not wearing sensible shoes to church, if my clothes are trendy instead of looking like a librarian, and if my purse isn't cleaned out every night. So don't spend every moment trying to be perfect. The truth is, no one thinks about you as much as you do, so be crazy every once in a while.

Your confidence should come from God; and the talents and skills He has blessed you with should be honed and crafted for His glory. I have found that trusting in God is a safe place to rest. After all, if God is for us, who can be against us (see Rom. 8:31)?

What dream has God placed on your heart? What talents has He blessed you with? I thought I'd been passed over in the talent department until I realized that not all talents are showy, like dancing and singing. Can you cook? Do you like to write? Do you

...am of building the next skyscraper? Honey, whatever passion you have, follow it. Be proud of what you're good at, and never fall short to please anyone.

Pride in your work is not the same as boastful pride. When we excel in using the talents God gave us, the Bible says He's willing to bless us more (see Matt. 25:14-30). When we do our work to give God the glory (see 1 Cor. 10:31), He is willing to bless us *immeasurably* more (see Eph. 3:20-21). Go after your dreams and let your man find you doing what you love.

## Wait for Mr. Right

Part of trusting in God means waiting for Him to bring the right man to you instead of looking for Mr. Right on your own.

God did not bring Prince Charming to me in high school, which is a blessing. If Justin and I had attended high school together, there is no way we would have ended up at the altar. Not with each other, anyway. We both had a lot of refining that needed to happen before our paths could cross successfully. I'm thankful that I serve an all-knowing God who told me to wait when I prayed to meet my soul mate.

We think that being single in high school carries a certain . . . "loser quality," which is a totally stupid belief. Why did I think I needed someone to like me? To tell me I was pretty? Why did I crave that attention? Maybe I was simply tired of walking around during the lunch period to avoid the accurate perception that I didn't have anyone to eat with. I was lonely.

I didn't want to wait for Mr. Right, so I settled for "Mr. Not Right for Me."

Four cute guys sat in the back of biology class, and Sean Campbell was the cutest—tall, dark and ruggedly handsome. A real "man's man." Testosterone dripped from his pores.

I had a huge crush on Sean, but we never talked to each other. One of the other cute boys, Derek, walked around with me on a field trip, thus ruining any shot I had with Mr. Wonderful. Looking back, I never had a chance with Sean, but a girl could dream.

This is where confidence is of the utmost importance. A confident girl does not date a guy just because he likes her. She remains single until the guy she wants decides he wants her.

A confident girl does not date a guy just because he likes her. She remains single until the guy she wants decides he wants her.

But, I wasn't confident.

I wanted to be in a relationship so that I wouldn't feel so alone. Having a boyfriend was a status symbol. So, I started dating Derek, and I became somebody. Unlike me, he grew up with most of the kids at our school, so he was well known and well liked. Derek was smart and came from a respectable family, and I thought he was cool. I no longer had to search for someone to eat with at lunch, and I had a ready-made lab partner. But were these the right reasons for dating Derek?

The Bible says that "the heart is deceitful above all things. . . . who can understand it?" (Jer. 17:9). I thought I knew my heart, but my "love" for Derek was a lie. After tasting the richness and depth of my love for my husband, I see how silly I was back then. I am sorry for my part in it. Derek is now married to the love of his life, and I'm thankful that we both found our heart's desire.

Unfortunately, when your confidence isn't tied to Christ, it's anchored to something else. A boyfriend in high school can be a major weight, dragging down a girl's heart, encumbering it from the heights it could reach.

Instead of focusing on friendships with girls, I unknowingly alienated myself from them. Instead of nurturing my faith in Christ, my spare time was spent in the drama of a teenage relationship.

Even if you're blessed to marry your high school sweetheart, your perception changes as you age; and when your love naturally intensifies to an adult level, you can agree that the high school time was full of infatuation that deepened to something more.

It's a definite red flag when a couple gets too close too fast, primarily because while girls wrap themselves fully in their relationship, guys aren't as willing to lose their identity. You don't see many guys doodling "Mr. and Mrs. So-and-So" in their journals. Although Justin did find an old high school notebook where he'd written "Justin loves Katrina" in the margin. *Awwww*. Barf.

Being Derek's girlfriend became part of my identity. It was special to be "taken" or "off the market." I'd given up on Sean due to the "bro-code" which wouldn't have let him date me after his friend, and there wasn't anyone else in my high school I wanted to date.

My high school yearbook is full of people bidding me a happy summer and a great wedding to Derek, even though we were nowhere near being engaged. We'd broken up and "gotten back together" sooooo many times. Some of our friends nicknamed me "Mrs. Thatcher" and addressed me that way in their farewell adieus. Instead of our friends knowing *me*, I'd hidden myself behind him. But God didn't create us to stand behind our men; He created us to be equals.

## Purposeful Singleness

After I'd gone to college, a lady at my church gave me a dating book she'd bought for her daughter. I devoured it. Derek and I attended the same college, unwilling to let go of what was familiar, unwilling to let God work in us independently At least, that's how I felt. After inhaling the book *I Kissed Dating Goodbye* by Joshua Harris, I broke up with Derek for good. And, thankfully, instead of feeling lonelier, I felt freer.

Harris talked about purposeful singleness—that there is a benefit to choosing to remain single while waiting for God to reveal His purpose for us. I loved the idea but found it hard to not "rebound" after a long relationship. My first attempt at purposeful singleness was an epic fail.

Even though we were broken up, I still spent a lot of time with Derek and got to know his roommates. I had a crush on Brandon, and we ended up sort of dating. I don't really even know what to call it. But I pursued him when I probably should have just left him alone.

Pursuing a guy leaves you as the one most vulnerable to getting hurt. How do you know if he really likes you? The first year away from home is filled with figuring out who you are. Bringing boys into the equation can really mess with your head.

After transferring to a college closer to home, I tried my second attempt at purposeful singleness. I got a job at a local hospital. I woke up every morning at 5:30 and ate scrambled eggs with ketchup (*the only way to eat eggs*) in the hospital cafeteria while reading my Bible before my shift started. I'd like to say that I declined offers from eligible suitors, but I didn't have any "romantical" offers for almost a year. I think God didn't trust me yet.

It was during this time that God became more real to me than He ever had before. I grew closer to Him; and though my loneliness was a constant hurt, I had peace like I'd never experienced.

Sometimes God removes you from your dreams so that
He can give you something better.

Sometimes God removes you from your dreams so that He can give you something better. I still wish I had a diploma with the Florida State University logo on it, but when those jealous twinges hit, I twirl the bands on my left ring finger and thank God for leading me out of Tallahassee.

Church became my haven. I was now a sponsor with the group I had graduated from a year before. My friends were my youth minister, Mark, and his wife, Stacey, and the kids in our youth group. I would drive almost an hour to church every Sunday and Wednesday. It was pathetic from a social standpoint, but God was preparing me. Meeting Justin was only a year away.

I'd found my confidence again. I was a leader and role model. I had purpose, and my home church family welcomed me back with open arms. But there's a difference between finding confidence in Christ and finding confidence in your church. Still, I was happy, and praying for God to reveal my husband. I'd been single for almost two years and I thought I was ready.

## Support System

I spent a lot of time with Mark and Stacey. We'd watch *Family Feud* or *Street Smarts*, and eat our "favorite snack" (graham crackers in milk). When Mark would recline in the rocker and declare PN time, that meant for 20 minutes no one talked while we all took Power Naps in our respective seats. They often invited me to come over for dinner, and sometimes I would stay the night. Their home was a sanctuary during times when mine felt like a tense courtroom.

Mark joked that they would have to adopt me, and the thought of being part of their family made me feel on top of the world. My confidence level was still hugely wrapped in the perception of others and tied with a ribbon of self-doubt. I needed to untie that bow and pour God's Word into my heart. If only we could see ourselves as He sees us, what a better world this would be!

Mark had an extremely impactful role in my life. My own father is brilliant—a Bible scholar with degrees, awards and language-interpreting skills out the wazoo. He taught me that God's authority is final, and he instilled in me a deep love of knowing and understanding God's truth. As I got older and spent more time away from home, Mark filled in as a surrogate father figure. After I returned home from college, I asked him to be my "authority" on guys, because it was easier for him to gauge a guy's character than for me to bring guys home to meet my family.

It is imperative to find people in your life who can tell you hard truths—people who will look out for your best interests. Along with Mark and Stacey, Bonnie was my main support system when I met Justin. She was my "wing woman," and through our mutual friendship, she helped Justin and me navigate the awkward waters of getting to know each other.

## Wait

Sometimes God doesn't reveal our Prince Charming right away. Why would God give us someone to compete with Him? When we can't love God first and most, we're unable to love someone else the way we should.

When you love God first, you agree that He made you as an amazing creature. You are a woman! Be proud. Be strong. You are awesome by the very nature of being female.

Wait for the man who sings to you in the grocery store aisles to the music playing softly in the background. Wait for the man who takes your breath away with a moonlit stargazing session on the campus field late at night. Wait for the man who makes you feel adventurous but wraps his arms around you on your first Jet Ski ride because you're terrified of the dark water's depth. Wait for the man who shows off on your private stretch of beach by diving off the back of said Jet Ski and losing his favorite watch.

Wait for the man who makes you feel invincible and protected at the same time. The man you'd step onto a magic carpet for.

God made us the crown of His creation, the incredible culmination of an impressive, mind-blowing work. Why do we let people put us down? Why do we let guys treat us like trash?

Eleanor Roosevelt said that no one could make you feel inferior without your consent. It's a nice thought, but I'm not sure it's true. I can feel inadequate just by being underdressed. Plus, some girls are just mean. I don't have to show them I'm hurt, but the damage is done nonetheless.

My friend Kaylee is one of the most gorgeous people I know. Her dark hair and prettily angled features remind me of Victoria Beckham. She's determined, smart, kind, thoughtful and loyal.

Basically, she's awesome. But she never saw herself that way. I don't think she ever saw herself as "good enough." She went through a few years of partying and drinking; but after getting pregnant with her daughter, at 18, she changed her mindset.

She lost her confidence for a while, but she didn't stay in that place. She remembered who God created her to be. Instead of looking for a guy to support her, she took charge of her life. Instead of letting insecurities victimize her, she attended church and enrolled in the police academy.

She's now a successful police detective, and married to an incredible man. She's living her happily ever after.

My happily ever after started after I made God the center of my life. I was closer to Him than I had ever been. My two years of "purposeful singleness" taught me a lot about who I was, and I was so eager to start living my life. I was ready to be on my own but felt stuck in a daily routine of normalcy and boredom.

I desperately wanted to meet the love of my life; and because I believe that God won't bring two people together until they're both ready, I decided not to be the one holding up the process.

I desperately wanted to meet the love of my life; and because I believe that God won't bring two people together until they're both ready, I decided not to be the one holding up the process. So I studied my Bible. I led Sunday School classes. I communed with God like He was my best friend in the most respectful of ways. Then and now, I talk to God pretty much all day in my head, like He's an invisible friend on my shoulder that only I can communicate with. I know that He doesn't care if I can't find my headphones or if my makeup looks good, but He cares that I care.

Something interesting happened during this time. While I never stopped looking my best in case I met my dream guy, and I never stopped daydreaming of the how and why of our first encounter, my relationship with God and my work at the church became my priority. After I stopped worrying about meeting the love of my life, God led Justin to my office. *Wait 'til you hear that story!*

I was now confident in who I was, and that shined through.

Justin wanted me the minute he laid eyes on me.

Confidence is sexy.

Confidence is found in Christ.

# 2

## *Preparation*

*Be still before the LORD and wait patiently for Him.*

PSALM 37:7

I read a poem when I was in college that depicted God with arms outstretched, holding a man and a woman in separate hands. He kept His hands apart until both the man and the woman were looking at Him. Focused. Intentional.

If only one of them was looking at Him, His palms remained apart until the other person also turned toward Him.

Palms face up, He drew them closer to each other as they remained focused on His face, until His hands touched, and they were united with the love of their life.

From the moment I read that poem, I knew that I was not going to be the reason that I hadn't met my future husband. I had to make God the focus, the center of everything in my life, before He would bring my love to me. God didn't need a rival. If I had to wait to meet my husband, it would be because *he* wasn't ready.

I waited two years for God to orchestrate that meeting.

Looking back, it was no coincidence, no fluke or happenstance that brought Justin and me together.

Three months before we met, God began directing.

The stage lights flickered and hummed. The gears engaged and creaked as angels prepared to draw back the curtains on our love affair.

## Friends First?

I like the popular song "Lucky" by Colbie Caillat and Jason Mraz, but I'm not sure I love the line that says "I'm lucky I'm in love with my best friend." It's popular advice, and it's said out of a necessity to understand the specialness of the connection. In a sense, Justin *is* my best friend, because he's the one I trust with my deepest secrets, my insecurities, and my fears. But on the other hand, there are things that you just shouldn't talk about with your man because, to be blunt, he cares but he doesn't care.

The deepest part of my soul recognizes Justin as so much more than my best friend. Any extra explanation after introducing him as my husband is unnecessary. It's almost like it's a given quality that doesn't need to be said out loud. Justin has always been more than my "best friend," but he definitely didn't start out that way. It was instant attraction, instant connection and instant desire. We weren't friends first.

Some great friends of ours were lucky enough to find their true love in high school. They've had the privilege to "grow up" together and watch each other mature. Their stories are filled with memories of each other's most awkward moments, precious to them, and funny to everyone else when they share their stories.

Your boyfriend shouldn't be your *only* friend.

Whether your guy turns out to be the guy you grew up next door to your whole life, or a stranger you locked eyes with while getting off the subway, a foundation of friendship needs is a necessity. But keep in mind that your boyfriend shouldn't be your *only* friend. Sometimes best friends get married, but honey, I want you to have girl best friends. I want him to have guy best friends. And I want you both to be more than each other's best friend.

There are things that girls need to talk about that guys don't ever want to hear! Girlfriends are *so* important—even critical—to having balance in your relationship with your guy. You want to look for best-friend qualities in the guy you marry, but choose to marry someone who is *more* than just a best friend

Set aside some time to do things on your own. Let him play video games with his friends while you have a girls' night. He'll be thankful you have someone to discuss "girl-only" stuff with. I promise.

## Prepare Your Heart

Before you meet your man, let's talk about laying some groundwork for how you'll react when it comes to the "baggage" he might carry.

Have you prepared your heart for the amount of sexual experience your guy might have? Does his sexual past become a deal breaker? Do you want to be equally matched experience-wise?

Let's reflect on Queen Esther from the Bible. She was innocent, pure, chaste. How scared she must have been—taken from her family and forced into a beauty pageant and about to spend the night with a king, whose sexual appetites left him with a long list of one-night stands and more experience than any one man should have.

This was not how she expected her first time to be. Thankfully, her year of skin treatments and beauty regimens gave her time to prepare her heart for what she was about to lose.

Part of preparing yourself for your happily ever after is reconciling in your heart that the man your heart desires might have given himself away before he met you. While I was saving myself for my wedding night, I had allowed inappropriate touching while I was dating Derek, and the guilt and dirtiness of that sin made me resistant to be with someone perfect.

One night, as I was thinking about my indiscretions from high school, God placed on my heart an overwhelming peace. I was no longer determined to marry a virgin. In my heart, I knew the likelihood of marrying a virgin was slight, and in a strange way, I forgave my future husband for any past mistakes.

I didn't want to have more experience than my future husband, even though what I did was extremely mild in comparison to most teenage relationships today. However, God's standards meant more to me. And compared to Him, I fell far short. I knew I'd have to confess to the man I eventually married. Not only did the thought embarrass me, but it also saddened me.

You may be in a similar situation. Maybe you've gone farther sexually than you should have and still feel guilty about it, even though you know God has forgiven you. You wish God would take away the shame. You may feel that confessing to God was easier than having to tell your future spouse face-to-face. I get it.

Here's the silver lining: You don't have to share your sexual baggage up front. In fact, I'm telling you *not* to share right away. Of course, I'm assuming (hoping) that you're choosing to wait to have sex until you're married.

So don't spill your secrets until he's proven worthy of keeping them. Just think how it would be to bare your soul too early and then break up. *Uh-oh*. Your ex knows your secret, and he just might share it.

*Hmm-mmm. No.* This is why we keep our pretty little lips shut. If he has indiscretions to get off his chest, let him. Unfortunately, not many people care if a guy has slept with his girlfriend; but if you've slept with a guy even just once, you can get branded with a sleazy reputation faster than you can blink.

So that night, as I lay in bed contemplating, I prayed for God to help my future love, whoever and wherever he was, to remain pure for me until we met. Prayer is powerful. My prayers for Justin coincided with the peak of his disobedience and his fall to the spiritual bottom. The earnest pleas I sent to God on behalf of my future husband did not fall on deaf ears. Even though Justin was deep in a sin-filled cesspool, he came out of it. He repented. He changed. I like to think my prayers helped him, because I know we serve a God who listens and loves us.

## Prepare Your Mind

First you prepare your heart; then you need to prepare your mind.

You do that by immersing yourself in Bible study and nurturing deep relationships with girlfriends, enjoying travel and hobbies. Get deeply engaged in your studies. Pursue a career. Enjoy your life.

After watching the movie *You've Got Mail,* and wanting to be Meg Ryan's character, Kathleen Kelly, I decided to read Jane Austen's *Pride and Prejudice,* Kate's favorite annual read. I got lost in the language, just as Kate described her experience. One of my favorite genres of fiction is historical romance novels set in the late eighteenth to early nineteenth century England. I love the period, the etiquette, the dialect. Propriety was of utmost regard, and manners were held in high esteem.

The 2005 movie version of *Pride and Prejudice* was not up to my standards when compared to A&E's six-hour adaptation. Colin Firth and Jennifer Ehle are worth all 21,600 delicious seconds.

Justin watched all six hours of the A&E series with me when we were dating . . . and not once since we've been married. Trust me, everything changes after "I do." (Wink.)

The ladies in Mr. Darcy's day were expected to be proficient in certain areas—what they called being "accomplished." The list of accomplishment included, but was not limited to, painting tables (*why?*), covering screens (*what kind?*), netting purses, a thorough knowledge of music, singing, drawing, dancing and the modern languages.[1] One of my favorite lines is when Mr. Darcy compliments the berated Elizabeth Bennett as she sits with a book in hand: "To all this she must yet add something more substantial, in the improvement of her mind by extensive reading."

After reading the list, I'm thankful that current female accomplishments don't involve all that studying! Our standards for success are different today, but what remains is the underlying thread of success called hard work. How many men are looking for lazy women?

Virtually none, I'd venture.

So the question begs, what do you want to be doing when your Prince Charming finds you?

Some princesses we've read about were minding their own business, focused on having a fulfilling life, while others were tied up in drama, curses and danger.

Snow White and Sleeping Beauty were snoozing. *How exhausting.*

Ariel was in the middle of a self-induced rebellion. *Only Poseidon can judge her.*[2]

Belle was in the middle of a rescue attempt when her prince literally fell for her.

Cinderella was immensely enjoying herself at the finest party she'd yet attended. She wasn't looking for romance or adventure. But wouldn't you know it? Romance found her.

· · · · · · · · · · · · · · · · · · · · · · · · · · · · · · · · · · · · · · · · · · · · · · · ·

A woman who can take care of herself is strong enough
to allow a man to take care of her.

· · · · · · · · · · · · · · · · · · · · · · · · · · · · · · · · · · · · · · · · · · · · · · · ·

Men are attracted to independent, smart, confident women. A woman who can take care of herself is strong enough to allow a man to take care of her. Remember, God created men to be protectors. It's in their nature, girls, so let your guy pay for dinner, buy you flowers and open your car door. Balance your ability to care for yourself with allowing your man to provide for you as well.

A man worth having . . . and keeping . . . is following the same advice I'm giving you. He's living his life, enjoying his friends and hobbies, pursuing an education and taking pride in his career of choice. This type of man is not interested in escorting a bimbo on his arm to business functions or introducing a trashy girl to his undoubtedly wonderful mother. So become the woman worthy of a man worth having.

## Perfect Timing

I love that God knows exactly when to bring you the love of your life. If I'd met Justin at any other time, we wouldn't have worked out. Before I met him, I still needed to gain confidence in who I was and what God wanted for me. After high school, I went to Florida State University for a year-and-a-half before God asked me to come back to my hometown. I worked at a local major hospital before transferring to the University of Central Florida (UCF). But the long drive, early hours and no social life were getting to me.

That's when things started to change. And God intervened in the most interesting of ways.

For the first time ever, my family had a Christmas dinner at a friend's house, instead of in our dining room. We dined with our preacher's family (his wife was, and still is, one of my mom's best friends). Turns out, Florida Christian College (FCC) had offered his wife a position as the receptionist and she'd turned it down.

Our host leaned closer to me and said, "Bethany, would you be interested in the position? It doesn't pay a lot, but they need someone to start right away."

I looked at my mom, who raised her eyebrows at me and smiled. We'd been praying for a job closer to home so I'd be available to pick up my younger brother and sister if my parents, who both worked an hour away, couldn't get home in time.

It seemed like an answer to prayer, so I told him yes.

"Good," he said, before taking another bite of gravy-smothered turkey. "I'll set up an interview."

I met Justin my first week at that job.

Justin's path to FCC was more intricate. He joined the United States Marine Corps fresh out of high school, following in his older brother's footsteps. He dated the same girl for a couple of years but found out she participated in an amateur's night at a local "gentleman's club" while he was away at training. To make matters worse, Justin's best friend was sitting in the audience. The next day, he called Justin and said, "Dude, guess who I *saw* last night."

"We just fought all the time," he says. "I believe now that we fought because our relationship was at a point where it needed to progress, but I wasn't ready to get married, period. And she wasn't a Christian. I guess I felt like it was okay to date her, but I knew that for our relationship to go any further, she needed to be. I knew I wasn't spending my life with someone who didn't have Christian values at the core of who she was."

They broke up for good soon after that.

Neither of us had been in a serious relationship for two years.

Neither of us were looking to date just to date.

Neither of us expected to meet the love of our life the first week on FCC's campus.

........................................................

"When I saw you, I fell in love. And you smiled because you knew" (Arrigo Boito).

........................................................

I love the quote from nineteenth-century Italian poet Arrigo Boito: "When I saw you, I fell in love. And you smiled because you knew." Looking back, that's kind of what happened with Justin and me.

He walked in my office and pretty much knew he wanted me. We don't call it "love at first sight" because there is so much more to love than the excitement of liking someone. How can you *love* someone at first sight? Instead of overusing the word "love," let's try a few different reactions.

Attraction at first sight.

Lust at first sight.

Infatuation at first sight.

Emotional response at first sight.

Physical response at first sight.

All of those things happened at our first meeting. Not love. Love came later.

Love grew into something amazing.

Love deepens and changes.

Love at first sight applies to when you see your newborn baby for the first time or hold your adopted child. Love at first sight pertains to your children, but not to your spouse. It sounds wonderful and romantic and dreamy, but love is more than feelings.

## Prepare Your Standards

Before and during a dating relationship, you've got to keep both eyes open; otherwise, you'll smudge your mascara. You are a detective. So observe your man. Know your man. Understand your man.

Everything he does while you're dating is like a crystal ball predicting what he's going to be like after you're married. If you don't like a habit of his, honey, unless you fix it before the altar, it's there to stay.

If he drives too fast, how likely is it that he'll slow down once you're married? Maybe he'll drive more carefully with a baby in the car, but you can't be too sure. If he's disrespectful to you about your job, finances, hair, clothes, friends and the like, it will not get better after you're married.

When Justin and I started dating, we agreed that if at any time one of us couldn't see marriage in the picture, it would be over. It was our promise that we were in this relationship with a purpose. I wasn't interested in wasting my time with a guy who wasn't interested in commitment. I wasn't looking for a good time, *even though dating him was so much fun*. If no-strings-attached dating is what you're looking for, you might as well close this book now.

You are worth more than being a girl who stays with a guy because she doesn't want to be alone. How a man treats you when you're dating is a great indicator of how he will treat you when you're married. If he doesn't see the need to get you flowers now, he sure as heck won't bring you any when you are married.

If he doesn't surprise you with trinkets or flowers "just because," consider marriage a predictable blend of flowers for Valentine's Day, your anniversary, and your birthday . . . if you're lucky.

. . . . . . . . . . . . . . . . . . . . . . . . . . . . . . . . . . . . . . . . . . . . . . . . . . . . . . . .

Insist on being treated like the special lady you are.
You should feel cherished, protected and loved.

. . . . . . . . . . . . . . . . . . . . . . . . . . . . . . . . . . . . . . . . . . . . . . . . . . . . . . . .

Dating is the time to set high standards. *You* are the prize. Insist on being treated like the special lady you are. You should feel cherished, protected and loved.

The more time (and honestly, money) he invests in you, the less likely he is to do something stupid to lose you.

One of my friends has dated some of the strangest guys. One guy, I'll call him Homestead Dave, seemed perfect—on the outside. Her eyes lit up when she talked about him. I prayed that he was the one she'd been waiting for. Everything was going smoothly. They went on a few dates, and then he ruined everything.

Homestead Dave was living with his ex-girlfriend.

Why, Homestead Dave? *Why?*

Then there was Doug, a friend of her boss. Definite chemistry. He found reasons to be near her, excuses to stop by. He flew a kite with her. Singled her out at dinner parties. Then one day, he acted like he didn't know her.

Goodbye, Dougie. Goodbye.

I saved the best for last.

Victor.

Ah, mysterious, elusive, can't-be-tied-down Victor. But his good qualities were the male version of my friend's. They laughed about the same stuff, loved the same restaurants and just had a great time being together. I was afraid Victor might be the one. She was pretty serious about him for a long time until she realized she couldn't pinpoint what his job actually was. *Entrepreneur* can mean anything. We Google-stalked him to no avail.

Then she found out he was still in communication with his ex-wife. Plus, his mother was overly dominant and treated this 32-year-old man like a child. Did I mention he might still be in love with his ex-wife? So my friend said goodbye, but that Victor was so magnetic. He was under her skin, and she couldn't fully let go.

Some people are like that—born with natural charisma flowing through their veins. It's hard to watch a friend with a wounded heart; and it's even worse to be the person going through it. Dating someone who is still in love with his ex-wife is a deal breaker; but actually breaking the deal can be difficult. Fortunately, my friend was able to kick that man to the curb.

You will probably meet a young man who seems like the one. But you must prepare your mind for situations like I've just described. Until a man is ready to commit to you, and you are fully aware of and have accepted his past, part of your heart must be willing to have one hand on the doorknob and one foot ready to pivot and run.

Know your plan. Protect your heart. Keep friends around you. Pursue godly counsel and accept wisdom from those with nothing to gain or lose based on your dating relationships. This preparation leaves you fully ready to accept the richness of the love God has waiting for you.

**Notes**
1. List of female accomplishments taken from Jane Austen, *Pride and Prejudice* (1813).
2. Spin-off of "Only God can judge me."

# 3

# Qualifying

*There are only two kinds of people who are really fascinating: people who know absolutely everything, and people who know absolutely nothing.*

OSCAR WILDE

Being in love with Justin was—and still is—like being the heroine in a fairy tale. Sometimes I look at him and wonder how I ever got so lucky to have found a man like him.

I read a joke online about a woman who found an old kerosene lamp on the beach. She took it home and started to clean it when suddenly a genie popped out. He grants her one wish only, and she can't wish for more wishes. She thinks long and hard, and asks for world peace.

The genie laughs at her and tells her it's impossible since the countries have been at war for so long. Pick something easier, he says.

She thinks again and asks him for the perfect man—someone who helps around the house, listens, likes kids, respects the environment, doesn't watch sports all day and is a fun, wonderful human being.

The genie stares at her and then says, "Let's go back to the world peace thing."

When I read that, I thought it was a cute illustration; but then I realized that I married "the perfect man." Of course, nobody's perfect, but I found Justin's flaws only added to his "perfection." And when I hear other wives complain about their husbands, I *know* I married the perfect man. Perfect for me.

There are more perfect guys out there—single, wonderful, loyal men who want a family and desire to be an awesome husband. Sure, there are tons of dirtbags thrown into the mix, but if you strive to become who God created you to be, and follow His will for your life, God will bring that man to you. It's not your job to find him.

........................................................

*If you strive to become who God created you to be, and follow His will for your life, God will bring the perfect man to you. It's not your job to find him.*

........................................................

## Keep a Checklist

One time, I made a list of the qualifications I wanted in a husband. Cute. Tall. Funny. Smart. Christian.

But I think most girls want that. What was to set the guy I wanted apart from every other guy who was cute, funny, tall, smart and a Christian? I had to really think about it. Over the years, my list grew more detailed. I don't remember ever writing down all my qualifications, because some of them sounded so shallow. Turns out, most of us have a list that we don't share with anyone for fear of sounding vain. But that is what separates us, what shows our individual preferences. It's okay to have a shallow list.

Do you want to know my ultimate shallow qualification? I wanted a man who was "cool" in the eyes of the world but chose to be a Christian. I wanted a guy who could hang out with anybody, whom everyone liked and respected. . . a guy who was popular and didn't use the church as a crutch or need it in order to have a place to belong. I wanted to find a guy who chose God because he needed Him. Because he wanted Him. Not because God was the only one left to accept him.

God delivered. Justin partied with the best of them (not an endorsement) but gave up that way of life for something better. Something eternal.

Break out your notepad and pen!

Keep a checklist of character traits you must be able to observe *before* you choose to date a guy. Similarly, keep a checklist of things to watch for *while* you're dating to make sure he's husband material. Dating is a lot of work; but by prequalifying guys, it makes dating *so* much more fun.

........................................................................

Dating is a lot of work; but by prequalifying guys,
it makes dating so much more fun.

........................................................................

I didn't want a guy who had ESPN blaring all the time or who insisted on watching pro football. (Go, Noles.) One of my best friends, Windy, had a list of no-no's: He couldn't watch pro wrestling and couldn't have a receding hairline.

Justin didn't want a girl taller than him, and she needed to be more athletic than dainty. *I'm 5'3"—one out of two ain't bad, eh?*

After my long-lived high school relationship, my list grew more specific.

*Cute* changed to *Other people besides me think he's cute.*

*Tall* changed to *Tall, but not like a beanpole.*

I amended *Funny* by adding, *Thinks I'm funny*, because I have a really strange sense of humor. Most people don't know when I'm kidding, and I see wit in things that most people don't laugh at. If I'm laughing, people are usually laughing at me. And I don't think a man exists who can make me laugh harder than my sister does.

For example, I grew up watching *The Three Stooges*. There is an episode where Moe, the guy with the bowl haircut, is wearing a fake Hitler-type mustache. Larry (wild, curly hair) is playing the violin, and with a flick of the bow, the tip of it pulls the mustache off of Moe's face. He looks startled, feels his naked upper lip and exclaims, "My personality!" *You didn't laugh, did you? Cracks me up every time.*

It's okay. My sister and I ROFL, but most people don't think we're funny.[1] Usually, they are laughing because we're in hysterics with tears streaming down our faces. My husband calls it cackling, but that word always makes me picture a green-faced witch with a long, crooked nose, and I don't think I sound like one. *Or look like one*. Anyway, I'd give more examples, but you'd roll your eyes, and I want us to be friends.

Back to the list.

*Smart* had to stay. In fact, it really meant that he had to be as smart, or smarter, than me. I don't mean that to sound arrogant, but I wanted a man I could have intelligent conversations with. When our kids were grown and gone, I'd be left with my husband for the rest of our days, and if we couldn't talk to each other, what a horrible existence that would be. Considering that God blessed us with three sons who will get married and leave (*tear*), my relationship with my husband is more important than ever.

I wanted a man who was handy and would help around the house.

A man who liked children.

A man who provided and took pride in his work.

A man's man.[2]

He had to love his parents, especially his mother.

He needed to respect people, whether it was the server at a restaurant or the person taking tickets at a movie theater.

He needed to tip well.

What's on your list? Take a few minutes and jot down some things in a journal or on a piece of paper that you can keep safe. It will be interesting to look back at your list and see how your future hubby scored and how your requirements may have changed.

## God's Checklist

As I grew more mature in my spiritual walk, the qualification *Christian* became *Stronger Christian than me*. When you're looking for a husband, you want him to be "head of the house" material (see 1 Cor. 11:3). I'm not suggesting that when you meet a guy, you need to go through each other's spiritual decisions year by year. And I'm not suggesting that your man has to have been a Christian longer than you. What I am saying is that the man you marry should be worthy of your respect and your trust, and have a relationship so tight with the Father that you are convinced beyond convincing that he will always look to Him first. You have to trust that he can handle the ultimate responsibility of leading your household spiritually.

As I continued to grow in my walk with the Lord, the *depth* of my future husband's Christian walk grew more important. We had to be of the same church denomination so that when we had kids, we wouldn't be fighting over christenings, baptisms or catechisms. More important, we needed to have the same beliefs on *salvation*. Once I admitted to myself that I couldn't date someone who wasn't 100 percent where I was, I knew it would take the hand of God to bring me the perfect guy. This was an issue we had to agree on, because every other issue rested upon it. If we believed the same about salvation, it almost guaranteed we would have the same beliefs about adultery, abortion and all the other hot-button topics.

Thankfully, Justin understood the extremely conservative family I was raised in. Both sets of our parents attended the same little Bible college in the same little town of Moberly, Missouri. It's a small world. Also, Justin understood the to-the-core faith I had in God and what the Bible says.

Does God have a checklist for your husband to be?

He requires qualifications for husbands and elders (see 1 Tim. 3:1-13; Titus 1:5-9), so measuring your standards to that list would be a good idea.

Jesus was clear when He said, "Don't be yoked together with unbelievers. For what do righteousness and wickedness have in common?" (2 Cor. 6:14). That means God says ix-nay on missionary dating.

A yoke is piece of wood attaching two animals to a cart so they can plow a field in straight rows. Typically, oxen of equal size would be used to plow fields. In this case, "unequally yoked" might paint a mental picture of an ox and a goat yoked to the same cart. *Are you shaking your head at this image? I am.*

An ox and goat pulling a cart would never result in a beautifully plowed field. It's the same as a Christian dating a non-Christian. If that makes you mad, and you're ready to throw down this book, that's fine as long as you promise to pick up another one—the Bible. Scripture is full of truth that can be hard to swallow, but God wrote it. Jesus said it. I'm just repeating it.

I'm not discounting situations where a believer leads her boyfriend to Christ. Amen and praise God! I'm not saying you shouldn't invite people to church. I am saying that Jesus said not to be *yoked* with an unbeliever; and if you're dating, you're getting ready to hitch on that yoke.

If you date a guy who is a Christian, you eliminate many of the vices typical in a non-Christ-centered relationship. And let's be clear with the definition of "Christian" here. As a youth minister's wife, I feel protective over the girls in my youth group. So when a girl starts dating someone, I get nosy. The first thing I ask is if he's a Christian, and her face says it all. Sometimes she smiles and looks away because he isn't, or she defends him to the extreme. "Oh yes, he goes to church and comes to our lunch Bible study."

That's not what I asked.

Going to church makes you a Christian the same way sitting in a garage makes you a car.[3]

. . . . . . . . . . . . . . . . . . . . . . . . . . . . . . . . . . . . . . . . . . . . . . . . . . . . . . . . . . . . . . . .

Is he sold-out for Jesus? Does he look to God
for his answers and support?

. . . . . . . . . . . . . . . . . . . . . . . . . . . . . . . . . . . . . . . . . . . . . . . . . . . . . . . . . . . . . . . .

Is he sold-out for Jesus? Does he look to God for his answers and support? Does he make church a priority because he's expected to be there, or does he go because he wants to?

If he's a Christian, he probably doesn't do drugs, drink (a lot) or smoke. If you date guys who don't drink, smoke, curse and sleep around, then you won't spend your dating time fighting about alcohol, cigarettes, foul language and cheating.

If he's a Christian, he has a positive support system, either with his family, friends or church. Someone is looking out for him, which means you don't need to mentor, parent or coddle him.

And most important, if he's a Christian, God holds him to a higher standard. I love that Justin weighs his actions based first on how God sees them and then by me. The Holy Spirit convicts him of things that I may never know about. *But sometimes I tattle to God about Justin.*

Admit it—sometimes our men need to be told on. Because Justin is a Christian, he understands the most important part of me. He has full access to my soul because he understands that God is more important to me than he is. And God is more important to him.

## Opposites Attract

Couples don't have to like all the same things. Justin and I couldn't be more different if we tried. I'm sometimes curious if we would have been matched up if we had made accounts on a dating website.

He's all outdoorsy, handy and technologically astute, while I'm a homebody, brainy and a Captain Safety. When I take a risk, I almost always regret it. When Justin takes a risk, he always wishes he'd done it when he was younger—"would have hurt less," he says.

Justin grew up surfing, skim-boarding and playing beach volleyball. I spent the majority of my childhood indoors. Justin tans. I burn.

He loves ironic movies, sophomoric comedy and Westerns. I appreciate cooking shows, reality television and dry humor.

He's crunchy peanut butter with strawberry jelly. I'm creamy peanut butter with raspberry jam. He's the Reese's to my Twizzlers; sandwiches to my pizza; buffalo wings to my pasta.

He's cocky; I'm insecure. He's outgoing; I'm reserved.

Justin's adrenaline gets pumping when he's faced with confrontation, and he doesn't back down from a fight. I freak out when I think someone's mad at me.

His coffee cup is half empty while my latte is half full. He's the king of making a deal, while I'm the queen of reading the fine print. He's the mischief I needed, and I'm the steadiness he craved.

Basically, I married Zack Morris.[4]

I'm definitely not Kelly Kapowski (TV Zack's girlfriend), but with Justin, I'm the best version of myself.

Besides wanting to be Kelly, I also wanted to be Kimberly, the Pink Power Ranger; DJ Tanner from *Full House*; and Topanga from

*Boy Meets World.* I didn't realize until I watched reruns of these shows how heavily these characters influenced the majority of my middle school fashion sense.

In my fantasy, I was charming, beautiful, funny—basically, any guy's dream girl. But when I looked in the mirror, I saw a stringy-haired academic with caterpillar eyebrows, big teeth and a too long face. I was such a tomboy that I didn't care about clothes, my figure or what I ate; but I'd kill to have that body again.

When it comes to the person you want to marry, being equally matched in terms of character, temperament and beliefs leads to peace in the relationship. Your deep inner convictions, ethics and morals should be reflected in that person.

Justin and I are extremely different, but our commonalities are strong on the things that truly matter—faith, family and politics! We teasingly bicker about what to watch on Netflix, and we high-five when we try a new show and both like it. It's okay that our hobbies and interests aren't the same, because our foundational convictions are identical.

Windy's husband is an ESPN fanatic. Sports 24/7. At first she hated it, but now she plays her own Fantasy Football League and makes snacks and goodies on game day. You can learn to appreciate each other's differences. It helps you to widen your horizons. Similarly, I'm about to learn how to play golf so that I can enjoy an activity with my man. Never feel that you have to marry someone like yourself—if you were completely alike, one of you wouldn't be needed!

The bottom line is this: When a man worthy of pursuing you enters your life, take notice! He's a catch!

## You Don't Fall in Love

After we'd been officially dating for a couple of weeks, Justin took me on a mini-date. It was moments past twilight, and the small college was blanketed in an unusual quiet. The dorms were built close together, with the original set facing each other in two half-moons shapes. The small lake bounced the moonlight off its still surface and the woods at the back of the property were not fearsome when Justin was holding my hand.

He led me to the outer rim of the campus that led to a giant field and opened the sleeping bag he'd draped over his arm. He unzipped all the edges and spread it out on the cold grass. The light from the street lamps gave enough glow to prove to anyone who might look out their window that we weren't being inappropriate; but since I was an employee, I knew this type of fraternization might be frowned upon by the administration.

I live too much inside my head at times, and while Justin was totally calm and debonair, I was a nervous wreck, trying to appear collected while my heart raced and I constantly checked the perimeter.

He lay on his side, head propped by a muscular arm, and I mirrored him—a respectable amount of space between us. Save room for Jesus.

It scared me how much I liked him. I knew I was entering life-changing territory with Justin. I didn't want to be another notch in his belt or just another girl to him.

> "You don't fall in love, you grow in love. . . . If you fall in love, you can fall out of it. We'll let love grow."

I was already falling for him. And that frightened me.

"Don't let me fall in love with you," I whispered. I was baiting him. His response would tell me a lot, but he said something I never expected.

"You don't fall in love, you grow in love," he said. "If you fall in love, you can fall out of it. We'll let love grow."

## Special Places

There are few love stories, either in books or on the big screen, that truly capture my feelings for Justin. I understand Bella's obsession with Edward from *Twilight*, and Noah's agony after losing Allie in *The Notebook*. I couldn't get enough of Justin and still can't.

We used to get away from campus by jogging at our city's lakefront. We usually didn't run as much as we'd sit on the dock and talk while the sky turned pink and purple as the day woke up. I hate getting up early; but when the alarm buzzed, I was out of my house in 10 minutes, not wanting to waste a precious second of time with him.

The lakefront was our special place.

We'd sit on the one lone swing and talk forever, learning about each other. Sitting close to each other and enjoying just being together. Perfection.

There are so many things about the man I chose to marry that I never thought to put on the list. Interestingly, many of the attractive parts about Justin were traces of people I'd had crushes on in the past.

The way his tennis shoes are always untied with the laces tucked in. His no-show socks (*the man has sexy ankles*). The way he wears a baseball cap or a bandanna when it's hot. How he smiles at everyone, but when he reaches for my hand, I'm the only person in the room.

When you meet a potential boyfriend, your brain subconsciously starts ticking off the qualities one by one. When he passes the major criteria, the hallelujah chorus rings out. When he's romantic and buys you presents, tries hard to win your favor and whispers sweet words in your ear, you can be head-over-heels for him. And if he values God's opinions over yours, honey, you've got yourself a winner.

## David and Mallory

I've been blessed to watch students from our youth group graduate, chase their dreams and grow in love with their beloveds. David and Mallory, a couple who "did it right," are reaping the rewards as newlyweds.

Mallory's Advice: Set those standards HIGH, and don't let anyone alter them. There is someone out there for you, but be patient and wait for the right one. Don't waste your time dating guys you wouldn't even consider meeting at the altar one day. Believe me, when you do find the right one, you'll know, and he will be totally worth the wait!

**Notes**

1. Just in case you needed to know: ROFL stands for Roll on the Floor Laughing.
2. Think "The Rock" or Channing Tatum (minus the stripping).
3. This is a quote from Billy Sunday (1862–1935) that I've loved it for years.
4. A main character in the TV sitcom *Saved by the Bell,* which aired between 1989 and 1993.

# 4

# Positioning

*The instinct of a man is to pursue everything that flies from him,
and to fly from all that pursue him.*

VOLTAIRE

I had a crush on Ryan when Justin entered my life.

I ate lunch with Ryan, taught Bible studies with Ryan, sponsored youth camp-outs with Ryan and took guitar lessons from Ryan. I thought Ryan liked me, too, but he didn't ask me to the Heart's Day Banquet, though he did buy me flowers on Valentine's Day.

Justin helped Ryan pick them out.

Later that day, Justin asked me for my phone number.

Later that evening, Justin took me on our first date.

Justin didn't mess around.

· · · · · · · · · · · · · · · · · · · · · · · · · · · · · · · · · · · · · · · · · · · · · · · · · · · · · · · · · · · · · · ·

A man will do what a man wants to do.

· · · · · · · · · · · · · · · · · · · · · · · · · · · · · · · · · · · · · · · · · · · · · · · · · · · · · · · · · · · · · · ·

Chasing a cutie puts you in the driver's seat of the relationship; and honey, I'm telling you the passenger seat is a much better place to be. Think about it: You can't read, paint your nails, text or sleep when you're driving (*and if you do, STOP!*). There's no pressure as a passenger. There are no decisions to make, and you're not responsible for the lives of the other people in the car. No stress!

Notice that I didn't chase Justin. I was hanging out with *another guy,* but that didn't stop Justin from finding out about me.

When he saw me walk across campus to Ryan's apartment on my lunch break, he said to himself, *Who is that girl? Why is she eating with him? Why isn't she eating with me?* And then he set out to make that happen.

A man will do what a man wants to do.

One afternoon, Justin bought a bunch of ground beef and made up a batch of his deliciously tasty hamburgers. He grilled them outside and passed them out for free. Guess who ate lunch with him that day?

When a man pursues, life is a whole different ballgame. You're the prize trophy, not the participation ribbon. You're treasured, respected and special. You don't have to wonder if he likes you, because he tells you. He shows you.

Like in chess, we need to be three to five moves ahead. We are the queen, the most powerful piece on the board. We move any direction as fast as we choose. We control the pace.

Don't be scared to live your life, thinking that Prince Charming won't find you. I was minding my own business when Justin started his pursuit. He didn't waste time. He asked my friends about me and then invited me to hang out. I loved how he chased me.

## Don't Play Hard to Get, Be Hard to Get

Sometimes a girl's presence alone makes boys nervous. If the guy you're crushing on doesn't attempt to talk to you, move on with your life. Keep living your dreams, fulfilling your purpose and hanging out with your friends and family. Sometimes going out with another guy is enough to make your crush move. *But don't date someone to bait someone else.*

Let's go back to Ryan and the Heart's Day Banquet, which was held a few days before Valentine's Day. He hadn't asked me to go with him, and for that matter, neither had Justin.

I did not ask either of them.

So I let a friend set me up with a guy from her church as my date for the banquet. Nick was cute, funny and smart. He also attended UCF, and that's what we had in common. That night, we got our picture taken at the entrance and went into the transformed gym.

Justin was wearing his Marine Corps dress blues and looked extremely handsome. He was onstage for a "dating game," which required the three male contestants to do a dance and answer a couple of questions. Based on the audience's reaction, Laura, the female contestant, would make her choice, and the lucky pair would receive tickets to dinner. Justin followed contestant number two's "worm" performance with "the robot." The audience roared, and I still tease Laura about how she had a date with my husband before I did.

After the banquet, I noticed Justin was still around, so I lingered for a few minutes as well. My date was talking to mutual friends, so I sauntered over to Justin and congratulated him on winning the game.

My heart was chanting, *Ask. Me. Out. Ask. Me. Out.* I was surprised at my uncharacteristic mean-girl mentality when I admitted to myself that I'd make an excuse to Nick in order to hang out with Justin. That's not the kind of girl I wanted to be.

Justin smiled at me, motioned with his head toward Nick and said, "So, who's your date?"

I slowly turned my head in the direction he'd nodded, like I hadn't the faintest idea of the person to whom he was referring. I elegantly swung my head back toward Justin, and my voice grew haughty and drawn out.

"Oh, Nicholas? He's an *acquaintance* of my *dear friend* Georgette. We attend the same *university*." (Because *university* sounds so much more *polished* than *college,* and I didn't *attend* the same *college* as Justin so I was *superior* in my choice of *education* because I went to a *université*.)

Who was I?!

Justin raised his eyebrows, shot unsuspecting Nick another glance, then looked at me and said nothing.

*Be the first one to leave*, I thought.

"Well, we're off," I said, my voice returning to normal. To let him know that I was cool and not going straight home, I added,

"I think we're gonna get some hot chocolate and take a walk. Goodnight."

I turned on my heel and walked slowly toward the group, hoping Justin noticed the sway of my hips as I calculated every step back to Nick. In my fantasy, Nick would wrap his arm around me and whisk me off as I glanced back at Justin, who longingly stretched out his arm at me as he realized he should never have let me go.

Instead, everyone kept talking, and eventually we left. Nick and I did get hot chocolate and take a walk, but while sitting on a bench in the cool night air, chatting about who knows what, we both knew this relationship was going nowhere.

A couple of days later, Justin stopped by my office, pointed at the picture of Nick hanging on the divider separating my desk from the office administrator, and said, "Why don't you have a picture of me up there?"

Surprised, I said the only thing that came to mind. "I don't have one."

"I'll be right back," he said, and walked out of the office. An hour later, he laid a picture he'd printed from his computer on my desk. "You do now," he said, and left.

I was glad no one was around to see my cheeks flush red. What did this mean? Was I supposed to hang it up? We weren't dating. Did he want me to take down Nick's picture? I figured he'd swing by after class with my BFF Bonnie in tow, so I thumbtacked the picture next to Nick's and wondered what this meant for our relationship. I liked Justin a lot, but I wasn't convinced that he was interested in me. But why else would he have given me a picture? Didn't he like a girl named Maggie? I was confused.

It didn't help my racing thoughts when one of the more popular girls stopped by my office to ask a question and spotted Justin's picture. Her eyes grew excitedly wide. Justin was one of the "most eligible single guys" on campus, or so I figured, since I constantly overheard conversations about him from other girls who weren't paying attention to little old me.

"Are you guys dating?" she declared more than asked, as she towered over me, stretching her pointed finger as close to the picture as she could get without leaning over my desk.

Completely lacking poise, I said, "Ummm . . . well . . . he just gave it to me . . . ummm . . . I don't know . . . exactly . . ." while she smirked at my discomfort. She turned to her friend with wide eyes and practically bolted out the door. What if it got back to Justin that I thought we were dating? I wasn't anyone special on campus, and certainly not someone a guy like Justin would be interested in. While I definitely hadn't implied that we were dating, she would probably misconstrue the whole thing. What if he heard and thought I was being presumptuous? I sank in my chair. The joy and wonderment of the past hour vanished as fear of rumors filled my heart.

The next time I saw that girl was after Justin and I were *officially* a couple. She was walking downstairs from the top apartments and saw us standing at the crosswalk with another couple. Justin's arm was around me as he absentmindedly stroked my long hair. I smiled at her as her mouth gaped and her friend led her away.

It was a small victory, but because I let Justin pursue me, I was in no fear of looking like a fool after we were official. There is no fear of rejection when you are the one being chased.

## Be Approachable and Mysterious

Just because a guy likes you doesn't mean he gets to date you.

*Whaaat?!* (I hope you said that like the minions in the movie *Despicable Me.*)

Do you like him? Is he worthy? Does he meet the criteria? He could be super-cute and you might like him back, but if he isn't worthy, you're not gonna enter his car. Catch my drift?

In high school, I liked this guy in my youth group named Will. His friends called him Tuna because on the first day of school, he ate a tuna fish sandwich during class. When the teacher asked him to stop, the other students, in true guys-are-weird fashion, started chanting, "Tuna! Tuna!"

We played Sardines (*what's with all the fish references?*) at an overnight church lock-in. Will was "it," meaning he had to hide first and everyone had to find him. Once you found him, you hid *with* him until there was only one person wandering around looking for the big group of people.

I found him first, because as I walked by, he whistled at me. So I hid with him behind a bunch of folding tables that had been stored in a classroom. My heart was racing, and I was hoping he'd hold my hand while at the same time I was praying he wouldn't kiss me. I didn't want my first kiss to be with him in a dark classroom during a game of Sardines. I also didn't think he would find it as special as I would, so I prayed he wouldn't lean over.

However, being that close to him made my skin feel electric, like my blood suddenly turned into an electric current, and if he touched me, I'd swear I'd see sparks. Nervous energy filled the small space, and I enjoyed being alone in his company for the few special moments before Daniel found us and crawled behind the table.

Over the next couple of weeks, I received a few love letters from Will-Tuna. I sincerely wish I knew where those letters were now, because I don't remember throwing them away. I kept them hidden in the box of *The Great Illustrated Classics* books so my dad wouldn't find them. Occasionally, I'd open the box, take them out of their protective sandwich bag and reread the tiny red words. Those letters made me feel special, and my heart warms at their memory.

He and I sat in the backseat of the church van a couple of times on youth trips and, of course, sparks flew if a bump made us brush into each other. One time he held my hand and rubbed my thumb with his. I kept my arm so still that it cramped, but I didn't move for fear he'd let go. He had incredible charisma—he made you feel like you were the prettiest girl in the room. He was tall and husky, and he made you feel safe. He had tough friends, and he was a little on the rough side; you knew if anyone messed with you, he'd punch his face in.

Unfortunately, the older he got, the rougher he became. As an adult, he moved away from the church.

It would have been super easy to have dated him. To have kissed him. To have made out with him. Even though we sometimes sat together in the back of the van (*don't sit in the back of vans with boys*), I didn't jump in and save him a seat. If he wasn't mindful enough to get on the bus first, or save me a seat in the church pew, I sat with someone else.

Never let yourself be taken for granted. If a guy wants you to sit by him, he'll save you a seat. If he wants you to hide with him in a dark classroom, he'll get your attention as you walk by. And if he wants you to think about him while you're apart, he'll write you little love notes you'll cherish until the day you move away and can't find them anymore.

He may think that flirting entitles him to full access to your life, but girlfriend, your love has to be earned. The only VIP pass is a ring on both of your fingers.

When a guy notices you, there isn't much you have to do to keep his attention. This is when being mysterious comes into play. He may think that flirting entitles him to full access to your life, but girlfriend, your love has to be earned. The only VIP pass is a ring on *both* of your fingers.

You do not need to show off. If a guy thinks you're cute, he'll be waiting for you to enter the room. He'll ask his friends about you. He'll gather the courage to talk to you. You need to give him the space and time to do so. Believe me, if he likes you bad enough, it won't take him too long to work up the nerve, because he won't want another guy to get to you first.

## Seek Positive Attention Only

When Justin was around, I attempted purposeful mystery. I didn't raise my voice, draw unnecessary attention to myself or flirt too much. I didn't announce my plans like I foolishly did the night of the Heart's Day Banquet. If he wanted my attention, he had to work for it.

One day, he opened a care package from his parents and brought a red Tupperware stuffed with homemade brownies outside to the picnic tables. He started passing out the treats to everyone, then shouted up at the guys on the far end of the second story walkway. He joked around as Bonnie and I walked past him to get to our friend's apartment.

He offered us one of his mother's famous brownies, "his favorite," which Bonnie accepted. He smiled when he looked at me, his dimples deepening when he held the container out. I dropped my eyes while saying "No, thank you" before looking up at him under my lashes. He flashed his dimples, and my stomach flipped. I remember being impressed at how he praised his mother's baking and his willingness to share.

Bonnie and I started walking to the stairs, leaving him to pass out his precious goodies. I didn't look back at him again until we reached the top. He stayed on the ground for a few more minutes before going up the opposite set of stairs and walking toward our little group.

He told me later: "I had to pass out the brownies to everyone so that I could casually offer one to the person I was totally into." *wink, wink*

Mystery—1, Obvious Flirting—0.

I was intensely aware of Justin and extremely self-conscious around him. I know now that when he's nervous, he talks about the military. That day was no exception. (*And neither was our wedding day; but that's another story.*)

While we were all outside my friend's apartment, he started talking about the "index card." Apparently, the space between your eyes and your forehead, to the bridge of your nose, is the easiest spot to kill someone who is lying down. You just step on the person's face with your big military boot. (*I stand corrected. As I read this to him, he informed me it doesn't matter if the person is lying down or standing up. So there you have it.*)

Then he tried to get Bonnie to be the victim. He playfully tried to pull her down, and she squealed, but I remained quiet, laughing at them but not drawing too much notice to myself. I wanted to make him work for my attention, and work he did. I was jealous that he was touching Bonnie, but I didn't join in their antics. He kept checking to see if I was watching, so I smiled at the right moments and let him hold my gaze for a couple of seconds longer than necessary before turning away again.

A guy who likes you will do anything to be near you. One time, I grabbed a stack of papers from the shred bin and timed it so I'd be done shredding at the exact moment Justin's class dismissed for lunch. His class *happened* to be directly across the hall from the shredding room; so as soon as the roar of hungry students filled the hall, I watched until Justin exited. He stopped talking when he saw me, smiled, and stared. Proud of myself for throwing him off-guard, I smiled at him, excused myself through the crowd and walked back toward my office. I could feel his eyes on me, and I relished the look of genuine pleasure he had shown when he saw me.

* * *

"The unfading beauty of a gentle and quiet spirit,
which is of great worth in God's sight" (1 Pet. 3:4).

* * *

You don't have to be all glitter, sparkles and fanfare. Pop up every now and then, toss a sweet smile his way and go about your business. You'll be catnip to a man who's got you in his sights.

If I'd acted silly to get Justin to notice me, he would have seen me as a childish schoolgirl. And I wanted him to see me as a woman. Don't think that any attention is positive attention—nothing is further from the truth. I'm all for my extrovert girls acting super extrovert-y, but there's a difference between being a "people person" and being annoying.

We all know someone who laughs at a crazy-high octave that causes people to turn their heads to see who is breaking the earth's sound barrier. If your laugh is loud, great; just don't exaggerate it. People who laugh overly loud are, on a deeper level, hoping that people will take notice of them. Look at me! I belong! I have friends!

Insecurity is why I want Justin to put his arm around me in public. It's why I want him to reach for my hand when a pretty woman approaches.

The last thing I want prowling around my man is a woman who thinks she spots an opportunity. Show no weakness! When those feelings of insecurity pop up, the last thing you do is grab at your man. If I reach for *his* hand, or put my arm around him, I show my lack of confidence. A woman marking her territory is completely unattractive, and no one can track the scent of female insecurity better than another female.

The attention we are looking for is often more quiet. It's his wink from across the room; the gentle placement of his hand on your arm during a conversation; his lowered voice as he draws you into a private tête-à-tête. Intimate attention is the goal here, and when you're drawing a spotlight to yourself, you remove the opportune moment for your guy to make his move.

## Long Distance

I'm not an advocate of starting a long-distance relationship. Key word: "starting." Justin and I were together long distance for almost a year when he returned to active-reserve status. It worked for us because we'd already been together for a year before he moved.

Several of our friends have experienced success in times of a long-distance relationship. Some of our friends have not. There are exceptions to every rule. But we do not live our lives by the exceptions. We live by the rule and congratulate those who made it against the odds.

Are you the exception? Maybe. But people can get burned trying.

The best way to get to know someone is through face-to-face contact and personal observation. My brother takes it a step further. He observes *before* he starts dating. He says he wants to know what kind of crazy he'll be getting into.

The more work you put into your relationship while you're dating equals a great return when you're married. I hear people say, "Marriage is hard," and "Marriage is work," while nodding their heads. My heart sinks when I hear those phrases, because I don't see my marriage that way. I don't mean that we haven't had hard moments—one "moment" lasted 18 months—but loving Justin is as easy as breathing, and the "work" is usually related to fixing my own selfish attitude.

With more and more couples getting matched online, it's critical that the majority of your communication and time together is not virtual. Otherwise . . .

Does he tip well? You don't know.

When he's in rush hour traffic and gets flicked off by the guy that just cut him off, what does he do? You don't know.

When a stranger needs assistance, does he come to the person's aid? Again, you don't know.

Knowledge of your future spouse's faults is a *good* thing. Being able to identify those faults and consider their weight is a necessity if you want your relationship to last.

I know there are couples who have had amazing whirlwind romances, gotten married weeks later and remained happily married. I pose a few reasons for this: (1) they met later in life after they were a bit established; (2) one or both partners were married before and are building this new relationship out of their "learned lessons"; (3) they got married in a time when people didn't divorce at the drop of a hat.

A girlfriend of mine met a few guys from her online dating site, and each one turned out to be plain old wrong for her. Conversely, another girlfriend of mine just married the guy she met online and couldn't be happier. It's becoming more and more common to find a mate online, but remember, you have to be careful. You need to patiently watch so you're not fooled after saying "I do."

# 5

## Attire

*Modesty answers not the crude how of femininity, but the beautiful why.*

WENDY SHALIT

Watch the sun's effect slink across crags and into every crevice as it bids the day *adieu*. Wonder at the deepening pinks, purples and grays before the day shifts to the moon's soft glow. Examine the magnificent apparel God has bestowed on the creatures of the land and sea.

I pay homage to His design every time I polish my signature "zebra-stripes" on my toenails.

God is a fashion designer.

Pantone, leading expert on color matching systems, has nothing on Him.[1]

With all the splendor God has bestowed on us, sometimes we get caught up in how we look, and we feel the need to show ourselves off. If we advertise with our bodies we'll draw a "special" kind of buyer. And by *special*, I mean *creepy;* and by *buyers*, I mean *dirtbags wanting to drool over girls who like to show off too much skin.*

A good rule of thumb: If it wiggles or jiggles, keep it covered.

## Watch How You Advertise

At a two-day church youth conference I attended as a teen, speaker Phil Chalmers gave an illustration on modesty that I have never forgotten. He used cars in his example. I'm gonna use fashion.

Have you ever seen a commercial for Old Navy? How about for JC Penney? Target? If I'd asked you to raise your hand for each one you've seen ads for, you probably would have just kept your hand in the air for all three. Of course we've seen commercials for those companies. I like to shop at these companies!

But what if I asked you when was the last time you saw a commercial for Gucci? *No?* Well, how about Prada? *Shaking your head?* Yves St. Laurent? The only place I ever see ads for those companies are in haute-couture fashion magazines. Why don't they advertise on television, where everyone will see them?

Because they don't have to.

Their brands are easily recognizable as luxurious, elite and expensive. They are associated with class.

I'll let Phil take over from here. Phil said, "Ladies, it's the same way with your bodies. The more skin you show, the more skin you . . . advertise . . . the cheaper, more common you appear. Anyone can have you. Anyone can own you. That's the message you send."

He paused and looked around the crowded room. "But when you cover yourself up and are modest, that's when you become expensive. When you don't advertise yourself, it shows that you know your worth, and your worth is great in God's sight."

His voice quieted and his tempo of speech slowed. "And ladies, that's what every guys wants."

I'll never forget that illustration. The more skin you show, the cheaper you appear.

Don't get me wrong, I'm all for enhancing our best features. Let's take breasts for example . . . or, as I like to call them, "the girls," (thank you, Stacy London and Clinton Kelly from TLC's *What Not to Wear*). As Christians, it seems like we're often encouraged to act like we don't have them. Like we're supposed to stuff them away and try our best to pretend they're not there. But I disagree. God gave us "the girls," and we should embrace the fact that we have them. But we don't have to wear ultra-low V-neck tops to show them off. We just need to find a healthy balance between celebrating what God has given us and not flaunting it in guys' faces.

Studies show that when women wear revealing clothing, the majority of men assume the intent behind that clothing is to arouse them and elicit sexual advances.[2] I don't know about you, but wanting sexual advances is a far cry from wanting to look pretty!

God created guys to respond to visual stimulation. Girls are more emotionally inspired. What this means for us is that while our revealing shirt may catch the eye of the guy we're crushing on, it will also capture the gaze of all the other men in the vicinity. Especially, the creepy ones.

A girl dressed immodestly will have more guys drooling over her, but they aren't looking at her with respect. And they certainly don't care about how smart she is, or about her goals, or who she is as a person. We all want to look cute, attractive and sexy. We want the guy that we like to think we look pretty, and yes, sometimes (a lot of the time) we want them to want us.

I remember a picture on Facebook a while back. In the top box it said, "What We're Chasing" and showed a muscular hottie with his shirt off. In the lower box it said, "What's Chasing Us" and showed an overweight balding old man wearing a grease-stained wife beater. For every hot guy who sees us, there are 50 weirdoes watching too. We're not looking to be pursued by every guy!

••••••••••••••••••••••••••••••••••••••••••••••••••••••••••••••••••••••••

## Is My Shirt Too Low?

Place your flat palm, fingers together, on your chest with the side of your thumb touching the bottom of your collarbone. If your shirt doesn't reach your pinky finger, it's TOO LOW!

••••••••••••••••••••••••••••••••••••••••••••••••••••••••••••••••••••••••

## Is Modest Hottest?

Modesty is sexy.

While the idea of a sexy woman may conjure images of bikinis, Victoria's Secret models or breast implants, we can be sexy in a business suit, jeans or even shorts and a T-shirt. The trick is to understand our bodies and knowing what type of clothes look best.

One of my favorite TV shows is *What Not to Wear*. Any time I see Stacy London and Clinton Kelly dressing a woman with my height or body shape, I take notice. What works for her will work for me. Just like Stacy and Clinton give their clients rules to follow, I want to give you some general guidelines to ensure that your outfits work for you.

## Tip 1: If It's Uncomfortable, It's Probably Immodest

Looking sexy while staying modest has a lot to do with how you feel in your clothes. You may look fantastic in those leather pants, but if you aren't comfortable in them, unease will show all over your face.

## Tip 2: It Doesn't Fit If You're Constantly Readjusting Something

Once you're dressed, you shouldn't have to constantly readjust. If you're hitching up your pants or fiddling with your top, it's probably on the too-tight or too-small side. This includes underwear. There are no-slide, no-rise, no-wedgie underwear for sale at your closest Wal-Mart. Give them a chance!

This rule also applies to bras. If your bra strap is constantly falling down onto your arm, readjust the strap length or invest in one that has a better fit. A good bra is worth the investment and can last a long time. Several stores offer free bra fittings—you may be surprised to learn that you're wearing the wrong size!

## Tip 3: Lose the Panty Line

Speaking of underwear, the name says it all. Under-wear. To wear *under*. To be invisible. With the many varieties of underwear on the market, there is never an excuse for a visible panty line.

My mother almost died when I came home from college with thongs in my laundry. If you're still living at home, wearing a thong is a conversation you may need to have with your mom if your family is conservative. However, thongs do take care of the panty line problem, as do Spanx.

## Tip 4: Skip the Short Shorts

Use the finger measure rule to check if your shorts are too short. While standing straight, relax your arms by your sides. If your fingers reach past your shorts, the shorts may be too short. (For tall girls, I know this seems unfair. A cute pair of Bermuda shorts will look fantastic, though!)

### Tip 5: Fit the Widest Part of Your Body First

I hear Stacy London and Clinton Kelly say this repeatedly: Make sure your tops fit well. A shirt shouldn't be so tight across the front that it flattens your chest (don't smother the girls!), and if it has buttons, there shouldn't be a gap where you can see inside the shirt.

If you're large-chested with a small waist, a problem several of my girlfriends face, my advice is to make sure the shirt doesn't gap or pull across your chest. Take it to a tailor and have them fit the rest of the shirt to you. It won't be too expensive, and you'll have a custom-fitted shirt, which will look FABULOUS on you!

Moving on to pants . . . those of us with hips and booty to spare may detest trying on jeans to find a pair that doesn't gap in the back or swallow our legs. But it's worth it to find pants that aren't too tight in the front (we don't want a spotlight on our lady parts), that do not gap in the back when we bend over and do not give us a muffin top. Again, using a tailor's altering skills is a great way to ensure you hit all of these essential fit rules.

### Tip 6: Make Sure Someone Can't Peek Down Your Shirt

Girls over six feet tall, you don't have to worry about this one. For those of us on the shorter side, we must be careful that our shirt isn't cut in a way that would allow a taller person to sneak a peek. For example, when you're looking straight ahead in the mirror, your shirt may be extremely modest; but if you lean forward a little bit, are the girls exposed? Is the cleavage extreme? This isn't something we normally think about, but we must.

## Special Situations

Some occasions call for special outfits—prom, homecoming, your wedding. Finding a dress that you love and that looks great on you is difficult when you consider that a lot of dresses have high slits, are super short, have plunging necklines or are backless. Special occasions allow some wiggle room (did I just say wiggle?) and we can find the perfect dress that makes us feel sexy without looking slutty.

Last year, two of my youth group girls came over to my house before their homecoming dance and I had the privilege of helping them select their jewelry. They looked absolutely beautiful. The necklines were a little more plunging than I would want them to wear to church or school, but they were entirely appropriate for the occasion.

It's totally possible to find great dresses that are on the modest side *and* in fashion.

Stylists agree that showing one area of skin is sexier than showing several. What this means is that if your dress is strapless, it shouldn't have a miniskirt. Or, if your skirt is a little high, your chest and shoulders don't need to be bare. If your dress has a V-neck or plunging neckline, it shouldn't be backless.

This is good news, because it can make finding a great-looking dress easier. Pick your best feature and look for a gown that enhances it. For example, if you have long legs, a slit in the skirt may be attractive. If your shoulders are awesome, look for a strapless dress, but keep the skirt length long.

Another special situation is what to wear at the beach. A one-piece bathing suit is not always the best option. Stretching a piece of fabric across your entire body leaves nothing to the imagination, especially in the downstairs region. A tankini or a well-fitted top and bottom separates can be much more modest since they will fit better and not enhance your lady parts.

Certain attire is inappropriate for every occasion: bra straps that show; thongs and underwear that appear above the tops of jeans; see-through skirts; short skirts and/or shorts; tight jeans; tight or low-cut tops. A girl may think she is looking all cute and "sexified," but in reality, what does her outfit say about her?

There are some things we girls can do to look cute but stay covered. Place a cami under a V-neck top to cover up cleavage. Tuck it into your pants to keep your lower back covered when you bend over. Layering will always make you look put together.

Proper use of accessories moves the attention away from any problem areas. In the fashion industry, this is known as the "rule of three." Three eye-catching accessories are all you need to pull an outfit together. Start with a basic top and pants or skirt. Add a cardigan, blazer or jacket. Use a belt to cinch in your waist. Throw on a pretty scarf or sling a fantastic bag over your shoulder to complete your style.

Make sure your skirt is long enough to sit in. When trying on a skirt or dress, sit down in front of a mirror. Cross your legs. How much of your thigh is exposed? Will it be impossible for you to keep from flashing the world when you sit down or get out of a car?

## God's Perception

We don't have to look like nuns to be modest. We are beautifully and wonderfully made. We appreciate God's craftsmanship by taking the time and effort to look presentable instead of rolling out of bed, grabbing yesterday's clothes off the floor and dragging ourselves to school or work.

The Bible describes many beautiful women: Queen Esther (see Esther 2:5-8); Abraham's wife, Sarah (see Gen. 12:10-13); Job's daughters (see Job 42:15); Isaac's wife, Rebekah (see Gen. 24:15-16); Jacob's wife, Rachel (see Gen. 29:15-31); and King David's wives Abigail and Bathsheba (see 1 Sam. 25:1-3; 2 Sam. 11:1-5).

We want to be beautiful on the inside, but we can't neglect the exterior. Don't buy into the myth that the absence of makeup or accessories brings you closer to God's throne. And remember, if we do our best to look good for our guys when we're dating, we need to continue to do so when we're married.

The higher the standard we set for ourselves ultimately results in the standard we're setting for our future mate.

We want to be pursued by a guy worthy of pursuing us, and we want to attract the best. The higher the standard we set for ourselves ultimately results in the standard we're setting for our future mate.

First impressions are important, and since I was eager to meet the love of my life, I made sure the first time he saw me I wasn't in a T-shirt and sweat pants, with my hair in a greasy ponytail. When I started working at the college, I purposefully did my hair and makeup every morning before work because I wanted to meet a guy who cared about the way *he* looked. To be honest, I did look super-cute that day Justin walked into my office.

It was the same with Cinderella. She didn't go to the ball in her filthy rags. Instead, she allowed her fairy godmother to clothe her in finery. Prince Charming was attracted to her looks first, but he fell in love with her personality. Inner beauty is irresistible. As they danced and talked, he was attracted to her spirit.

The Bible explains:

> Do not let your adornment be *merely* outward—arranging the hair, wearing gold, or putting on *fine* apparel—rather *let it be* the hidden person of the heart, with the incorruptible *beauty* of a gentle and quiet spirit, which is very precious in the sight of God (1 Pet. 3:3-4, *NKJV*).

We can have fun with jewelry, makeup, hairstyles and clothes as long as our inner beauty takes precedence. Have you ever known an absolutely gorgeous girl who was snotty and mean? How pretty is she after you spend a few moments in her company?

............................................................

Would Prince Charming have spent his every waking hour looking for a girl who talked dirty and dressed like a tramp?

............................................................

Would Prince Charming have spent his every waking hour looking for a girl who talked dirty and dressed like a tramp? Would he have scoured the countryside to find a woman who revealed everything about herself on their first date?

Heavens, no! He was drawn to Cinderella's beauty and her sweetness. And because she left in haste, with no explanation, he couldn't get her out of his mind.

He had to find her, no matter how long or dangerous the search. He had to marry her to keep her from running off again. And as we all know, they lived happily ever after.

Isn't that what we want?

God chose women to be His crown of creation, His spectacular finale after He wove the fabric of the brilliant universe, the celestial bodies, the creatures of the land, air and sea, and even after He breathed life into a handful of dirt and created man.[3] I love that God knew girls didn't like to be dirty! His splendid works were incomplete without Eve, so He took a rib from Adam while he was sleeping and created her. Then He called His creation "very good" (Gen. 1:31).

The poetic verse structure in the Hebrew text of Genesis 2:23 suggests Adam celebrated Eve's creation. In the same way that Adam rejoiced over his soulmate, no guy should be allowed to treat a girl as anything less than His royal princess. This treatment should be of the highest regard.

## Wrong Impressions

If we want to be treated like princesses, we need to act (and dress) as if we are worthy of a gentleman's affections.

I thought I had a handle on modesty. I didn't wear tight jeans, low-cut tops or shirts with inappropriate phrases or pictures on them, like cherries, lollipops or bananas. Basically, if a phrase or image could be taken to mean something sexual, I shied away from it.

My fashion sense was nonexistent in high school, but I had more freedom in college to experiment with my style. My roommate was extremely fashionable. She looked like a young Britney Spears (before the shaved head.) She let me occasionally borrow a couple of tops, although I didn't feel as cute in them as she looked.

On Halloween, my friend and I dressed up and went to a friend's house. His roommate thought I looked hot in my off-the-shoulder leopard print top and tight black pants. If I'd been promiscuous, there's a possibility we would have hooked up. (I just noticed "hooked up" is only two letters shy of "hookered up." Hmmm.)

It was the first time I'd put myself in a situation where something bad could happen because of my outfit. My Tarzan/Jane-inspired "costume" was not reflecting the shy, prudish Christian girl I was inside. This was not the pursuit I wanted, even though part of me desired to be the girl every guy lusted after.

Clothes define not only who we are but who we want to be. Like in high school, I was so desperate to be accepted that I wore my cheerleading camp outfits practically everywhere. The word "cheerleader" had to be visible somewhere because anyone who saw me had to know that I *belonged*. I was *in*. I was *popular*.

Even though I wasn't.

Insecurity is a wicked animal. Stroke it long enough and it will bite you.

## When in Doubt, Cover Up

Justin and I were still in the "talking" phase (you know, not really dating, but almost) when, one afternoon, I stopped at his workplace to see him for a few minutes. Before getting out of my car, I took off the cardigan covering my cute-but-not-work-appropriate spaghetti-strapped tank top.

My plan was for him to see how attractive I was. So I left the sweater in the car. He was outside, and I walked up to him feeling good about myself. We chatted for a few minutes, but I noticed that he was standing weird, and our conversation felt awkward. Then I realized he wasn't looking at me.

I asked if everything was okay. He told me he thought I looked pretty, but he was a little uncomfortable because he didn't know where to look.

*Oh.*

A guy who preferred modesty? My wounded ego was impressed, although as I retrieved my sweater, I felt embarrassed and totally awkward.

Apparently, shoulders are sexy. I know that sounds crazy, but guys are wired differently than we are. That's how God created them, and Justin didn't want to be tempted physically. He wanted to do things right.

Bottom line: It's not our place to put impure thoughts into guys' heads. We don't understand that the male mind replays images days after seeing a girl in a short skirt or catching a glimpse down a plunging neckline.

A guy friend told me that he was minding his own business at a gas station, pumping gas, when he saw a girl at the opposite station. She wore an extremely short skirt, and he couldn't get the image of her legs and the idea of what was under her skirt out of his head. He thought about it for a couple of days. "Those images don't just leave your mind," he said. "I wasn't even trying to look at the girl, either—I was merely glancing around." He ended up masturbating to remove the building tension.

> While guys are responsible for their thoughts, we can't allow Satan to use us as a tool to lead guys down a path toward lust, pornography and sexually impure behaviors.

While guys are responsible for their thoughts, we can't allow Satan to use us as a tool to lead guys down a path toward lust, pornography and sexually impure behaviors.[4] Even wearing spaghetti straps during a church service can throw guys off. Another guy confessed that one Sunday, he had trouble concentrating on Communion and the sermon that followed because the girl next to him had bare shoulders. He was wracked with guilt for not being able to concentrate, but unable to push his thoughts away since she was right next to him.

Ladies, we may never fully comprehend how guys think, but if they're telling us they can't concentrate, let's help them out. Grab a cardigan for church or work, or anywhere, and let's keep our skirts and shorts an appropriate length.

Modesty is an indicator of our confidence level. How we dress speaks volumes about what we think of ourselves. Take a few extra minutes in the morning to do your hair. Apply some mascara and lip gloss, and pick out an outfit that looks good on you without revealing too much skin. This glorifies God's beautiful creation of you and lets interested guys know that you expect the best. A guy wearing a stained wife beater won't bother with a girl who wears well-fitting, modest clothes, because she's out of his league.

A godly guy wants to date a girl who shares his values. If you want to be pursued properly, you must dress appropriately—just enough skin to be cute, but not enough to reveal the goods. Dressing modestly helps keep his mind from going into fantasy overdrive.

Remember, a guy's pursuit is with an end goal in mind; and girlfriend, we're taking that pursuit to the altar. Once you say, "I do," you'll be able to wear absolutely anything for him . . . or nothing . . . anytime you want.

**Notes**

1. Pantone is the self-proclaimed "world-renowned authority on color." http://www.pantone.com/pages/pantone/pantone.aspx?pg=19295&ca=10.

2. Avigail Moor, "She Dresses to Attract, He Perceives Seduction, *Journal of International Women's Studies,* vol. 11, no. 4, May 2010. http://www.bridgew.edu/soas/jiws/May10/Avigail.pdf.

3. "The Uniqueness of Womanhood: You are the Crown of God's Creation," Eunique, June 17, 2009. http://eunique.blog.co.uk/2009/06/17/the-uniqueness-of-womanhood-you-are-the-crown-of-god-s-creation-6323957/.

4. If you're thinking that I'm referring to masturbation, this is not a debate I'm getting into. I'm not trying to make a case in either direction.

# 6

# Femininity

*I don't need a bedroom to prove my womanliness. I can convey just as much
sex appeal, picking apples off a tree or standing in the rain.*

AUDREY HEPBURN

During my mandatory eighth-grade summer school session, I wanted
nothing more than to beat every guy in basketball and hide my
blossoming figure. I loved football and made sure everyone knew it.

My jeans were baggy, my T-shirts baggier. I didn't care to know
the difference between foundation and powder. Lipstick was a
dirty word, and the only time a brush went through my hair was
after a shower.

I threatened to wear jeans to my senior prom.

Now I can't pack for a weekend without having a bag for toiletries, hair supplies, makeup and shoes. I have three cosmetic
bags, each supplied with mascara, eyeliner, eye shadow and some
sort of foundation or powder. I love hair and makeup tutorials
(thank you, YouTube), and I find it relaxing to watch Netflix while
curling my hair.

The point is, I didn't care about any of that stuff growing up.
I was not a girly-girl, and while I might look like one, I still don't
consider myself one—although when I say that out loud, people
give me the crazy-eye. (*The crazy-eye being a close relative of the stink-eye.
You know it when you see it.*)

Femininity has more to do with our inner self, than with how
we look. However, I believe the more we tap into our feminine
wiles, the more they will manifest on the outside.

## Feminine Stigmas

Janine, one of the sweeties in our youth group, is a girly-girl, but she refuses to label herself as such. "There's a stigma to being 'girly,'" she says. "Guys think you're not as tough or as good as they are, even if you're an athlete."

She stereotypically loves fashion, shopping and watching sappy love movies; but for her, the word "girly" conjures images of a preppy, prissy, blonde Barbie doll wannabe.

Most girls I know who spend time on their hair, outfits and makeup love nothing more than coming home and jumping into sweatpants. Their femininity exudes from them regardless of what they're wearing. It doesn't fade with every outfit change.

I have a friend who looks beautiful no matter what she's wearing. Even in jeans and a T-shirt, she looks flawless, put-together, stylish. I'm totally jealous. I wish I looked like a million bucks when I left the house in jeans and flip-flops.

........................................................................

Tapping into our feminine side does not mean we change who we are. If you hate pink, then girlfriend, don' t wear it.

........................................................................

Tapping into our feminine side does not mean we change who we are. If you hate pink, then girlfriend, don't wear it. It's extremely hard for me to wear anything ruffled, even though I love ruffled clothes on other people.

Do not equate femininity with Elle Woods from the movie *Legally Blonde*. I like to live vicariously through characters like hers on the big screen, but in real life, I'm allergic to that much pink. And I don't have the energy to spend two hours every day on my hair and makeup. I'd rather have three.

Even the biggest tomboy can be feminine as long as she minds her manners, doesn't dress like a hobo or try to dominate her world. Femininity comes from a quiet and gentle spirit (see 1 Pet. 3:4). Even my loudest-mouthed girls have a womanly quality about them because they don't try to act like men. Stand up for your beliefs, participate in extracurricular activities and, most importantly, think for yourself.

Be proud of your double X chromosomes.

What does a feminine woman look like? Strength drips from her, leaving glistening pools of vivacity in her wake. She is secure in her womanhood. She doesn't feel threatened when a man opens her door or pushes in her chair. She doesn't have a nagging sensation in the bottom of her heart when a guy tries to be "the man" in the relationship.

Don't ruin the handiwork of a momma who took the time to raise her son right.

Think of femininity as running the gamut from tomboy to girly to prissy, and ending in diva. Just because a girl is a tomboy as a child doesn't mean she will be a pro wrestler when she's an adult. We evolve until we find our comfort zone, and for a lot of us, we even out.

My "girlieness level" moved further up the spectrum with each son I gave birth to. Instead of reverting to my middle school extreme-tomboy ways, I was pushed toward more girly things. For instance, I wore a headband to church last week. And I feel naked if I don't have a right hand ring on, or wear earrings. I have to wear mascara. But I love it all.

## Gentleness

I learn so much from the students in our youth group. Stephanie is the quintessential athletic-tough-suntanned-blonde-lifeguard type of girl. She wears her hair in loose natural waves or gathers the thick strands into a ponytail; she barely wears makeup, and she dresses mostly in tees, jeans, shorts and flip-flops. She is effortlessly beautiful.

I saw the feminine-tomboy combination when she was holding my five-week-old son. I needed to hand him to someone so I could hoist my post-pregnancy body off the futon in Justin's office.

She was sitting cross-legged on the floor, and as I handed him to her, I felt this strange serene feeling pass through me. She reached out her arms and cradled his tiny body close to hers as she carried on conversations with the other students. My son didn't stir like I thought he would when he transferred out of my arms.

I stopped for a moment, partially because it hurt my C-sectioned body to move quickly, and partially because I was stuck in the moment. The grace with which she gently lowered him to her lap, and the way her arms lightly rested on her legs caused me to stop.

No one else saw the beauty in her movements or felt the peacefulness that washed over me. No one else was touched at the sweetness in Stephanie's voice as she whispered to my infant. It was a moment I've pondered in my heart, finally understanding Mary as she treasured the delight of the shepherds and the angels over her own Son (see Luke 2:19).

Even more touching was my son's response to being moved. He stayed asleep. Content and safe, he remained snuggled in his blankets, protected by her strong arms. The moment lasted all of five seconds, but it made me question my own level of gentleness.

· · · · · · · · · · · · · · · · · · · · · · · · · · · · · · · · · · · · · · · · · · · · · · · · · · · · · · · · · · · · · · · ·

"Let your gentleness be evident to all" (Phil. 4:5).

· · · · · · · · · · · · · · · · · · · · · · · · · · · · · · · · · · · · · · · · · · · · · · · · · · · · · · · · · · · · · · · ·

I'd memorized Philippians 4:4-9 during my time at Florida State. Paul tells us, in verse 5, "Let your gentleness be evident to all." I printed the passage on a postcard and read it first thing every morning and last thing every night. Anytime I happened to glance at it, I made myself say the words.

I remember thinking, *Was I perceived as gentle, or was I considered hasty, brash and mildly aggressive?*

*Did God think I was gentle?*

The memory of that postcard tacked on a tiny bulletin board in my small dorm room flooded back as I now wondered, *Is my gentleness evident?* I didn't think it was.

Gentleness is the foundation for a woman's true beauty and is of great worth in God's sight (see 1 Pet. 3:4). I had to realize that all of my primping in the mirror meant nothing if I couldn't train my spirit to be quiet and gentle.

## God's Examples

I have a superpower. This is how it works.

I walk into a room my husband has been sitting in for hours, and looking straight ahead, I sense a presence behind me. The hair on the back of my neck tries to shift under my curls, and my skin starts to tingle. Slowly turning my head, I look directly at the intruder.

Pointing (*my family points a lot—it's genetic*) I say, "What . . .is . . . that?" My husband knows that tone of voice. Looking at me, he moves his eyes along my outstretched arm to the tip of my index finger, and then spies the creature that's been staring at him since he sat down. With a heavy sigh, he stops whatever he's doing, gets up and stretches his own hand out to kill whatever insect I happened to see behind me.

I am the bug-whisperer. Except they always die.

We have black widow spiders around our house, and one time I found one *inside* my home. It had a death wish. I was praying it hadn't laid babies. So, after I killed it (Justin was at work), I Googled them and found out some interesting info.

A spider's web is silky, beautiful and fragile, but it's stronger than steel on a pound-for-pound basis.[1] The strands soften or stiffen, depending on the situation. Paradoxically, when a strand breaks, the web becomes stronger, not weaker.[2] The beauty is in the design. (The black widow has a funnel-shaped web, just FYI.)

I want to be a spider web kind of woman. Now there's a superhero! Excuse me, I mean superheroine. Her superpower is amazing strength and fragility rolled into one sweet package. When negativity rips life's strands, God remains strong in our weakness. If God allowed the spider to build something so resilient, I know He's instilled in us the same gift.

When a girl is sure of herself, she doesn't need to "out-free throw" the guys. Although I enjoyed beating the boys in middle school, my motivation was childish insecurity. Never lose to a guy on purpose, though. It's okay to lose, but honey, you play to win.

When a woman is secure in her femininity, she knows that if part of her world breaks, the other areas grow stronger while God tackles the weakness.

Another example of the balance of beauty, gentleness and sheer strength is evident in the waters of the deep. Countless poems, songs and ballads have been penned and heralded by those in awe of *la mer*.

Living in Florida for most of my life has given me the blessed opportunity to see many a beach sunrise and sunset. *Mostly sunsets, since I'm not an early riser.* The beauty of the waves as they sparkle with the sun's pink and purple glitter is breathtaking.

But underneath the splendor of the glistening waves is a power feared and respected by those who dare trespass. Ask any survivor of a vicious undertow or a shipwreck. A deceptive calm on the surface belies the current flowing underneath.

........................................................................

A quiet strength is more powerful than showmanship,
and a woman who taps into her God-given feminine nature
can do so without fear of being weak.

........................................................................

As a Christian, your strength is rooted in Christ. Nothing can snatch you from His hand (see John 10:29). A strong woman doesn't show her cards or have to prove anything to anyone. A quiet strength is more powerful than showmanship, and a woman who taps into her God-given feminine nature can do so without fear of being weak.

God reminds us repeatedly that the things of this world are not like things above, and His ways are not our ways (see Isa. 55:8-9). He uses the weak to shame the strong (see 1 Cor. 1:27); and while sometimes we may feel the need to "act like men," we are stronger when we act like women!

I firmly believe that God created a woman for Adam because there is more to God than just a masculine side. Since we are created in His image (see Gen. 1:27), part of God is soft, gentle, graceful, delicate and fragile. Since we would never say that God is weak, feeble or frail, why do we attribute those negative connotations to ourselves?

Remember how God presented Himself to the prophet Elijah? He was not in the wind that shattered rocks and tore mountains. Neither was He in the earthquake that followed the violent wind. After the earthquake, there was a fire, but the Lord was not in the fire. After the fire came a gentle whisper (see 1 Kings 19:11-12).

God was in the whisper.

He didn't have to prove anything to Elijah, yet He demonstrated His power in the stillness. When we use the charms and graces we've been given, we validate that femininity is a gift, not a curse.

Some women will never take advantage of their full potential as they try desperately to be in control of every situation and (I'm gonna say it) act like the man in the relationship. Honey, his pants don't look good on you.

## Learn from Others

I've had a few wonderful women help me on my journey to womanhood. In college, my New Jersey roommate was a self-proclaimed expert on makeup. She taught me how to groom my caterpillar eyebrows. *(Danielle, I'm forever grateful.)*

My youth minister's wife, Stacey, taught me how to sculpt my features with different shades of powders and highlighters. Stacey is beautiful—she needed no sculpting, shaping or shadow. She always reminded me of Fran Drescher, with her gorgeous thick dark brown hair, cute nose and New York accent (minus the nasal whine).

During one youth trip, we girls had a sleepover complete with junk food, boy talk and makeovers. We leafed through makeup artist Kevyn Aucoin's books and practiced transforming our faces. Our room looked like a caboodle explosion.

It's amazing how a little mascara and a touch of lip color can change your entire look. You don't have to wear makeup to be girly, but some fruity lip gloss can make you feel pretty. And when you feel pretty, you act pretty. That's a fact.

One of my dear, dear, dear-hearts, Allison, was unyielding in her resistance to anything classified as "girl." She was tough, stubborn and bold. She loved playing sports and spending time in God's creation.

"I competed against the boys and won all the time. I loved it. It was super fun, and I had lots of friends because of it," she said. "I had friends in seventh grade who told me to stop dressing like a man, and that's when I started wearing cuter clothes. I still wasn't girly."

The stereotype connected to being a "girly-girl" repulsed Allison the most. "A lot of the girls in my high school who dressed cute were idiots. So I didn't actually think you could be cute and taken seriously. I did a lot of thinking about being feminine versus being girly. What I came up with is that girlieness is exterior and how you dress. But being feminine is about the interior and how you act. I did Bible studies on being gentle and kind. As a result, I stopped being so aggressive."

When she started dating her fiancé, Matthew, she noticed that he embodied the masculine role. She didn't have to fight for him—he was completely capable of fighting his own battles *and* defending her.

"Talking to a lot of godly women also helped me understand that part of the way God made men was to fight for women, to defend them and protect them," she said. "Matthew is really good at expressing his thoughts and feelings. When I get aggressive, he lets me know that he is capable of handling the situation and to let him prove himself. He's a gentleman and a warrior. It's wonderful."

Elizabeth, another woman I am honored to know, is the perfect balance of strength and grace. She has a no-nonsense attitude, and she gets things done. She has a Type A (dominant) personality, yet she is one of the most godly, feminine women of my acquaintance. She respects her husband, Fred, and has learned how to put him as the head of their household. They are more in love than most married couples I know.

She's counseled me over the phone when I needed encouragement and prayed with me when I needed to change my heart toward Justin. Find a woman in your life that you trust and reach out to her. Ask for her counsel. Admit your mistakes and listen to her advice. She will be a treasure to you and will help keep Satan from finding a foothold in your relationships (see Eph. 4:27).

## How-To

There is a story of a professor who enforced a strict dress code on exam days—men in ties and girls in skirts. He claimed that if the students dressed professionally, they would score better on the tests. And his records proved that scores went up. It's interesting how what you wear affects not only your mood, but your ability to think.

Even something as simple as updating your footwear can bring out your girly side. My first pair of platforms was these huge white vinyl wedges. I didn't ask permission before I bought them because, as we all know, it's better to beg forgiveness.

I'm surprised my parents let me wear them, but I suppose they chuckled to themselves as I waddled out, allowing me the teenage freedom to choose my footwear. I felt grown-up and beautiful. Those extra three inches made me feel like a model.

Learning to walk in heels was a must, though. If I was going to wear high shoes, I had to wear them correctly. I didn't want to slump around, so I taught myself how to walk in heels. Short steps are the key, here, ladies, and try to land on the ball of your foot instead of putting all your weight on your heel.

And no, high heels are not good for your feet, but they add length to your legs. At five-foot-three, I'll take every extra inch I can get. Don't gripe at me about the damage heels do to our precious tootsies—I wear flip-flops 80 percent of the time, which are also not the best. I can't win. Wearing cute shoes are my fashion sacrifice.

One thing that always makes me feel girly is wearing nail polish, but I hate when it chips, so my fingernails are almost always bare. Once a year, I put a topcoat of clear polish on them to spice things up.

My toenails, however, are never nude. I've graduated from solid polish to painting zebra stripes on my big toes. I've finally given myself permission to like animal print, and zebra is my beast of choice. If you've never been treated to a pedicure, this is a direct order: Go get one. Take this book with you and enjoy the relaxation that comes with having your feet treated to wonderfulness. Pay extra for the massage-y chair. And shave your legs before you go. At least to your knees. You'll thank me after.

If you're nervous about having someone touch your feet, or embarrassed at the state of your tootsies, don't sweat it. They've seen *and touched* much worse.

When I come home from a pedicure, which is not as often as I would like, I feel glamorous, especially if I let them do a French tip pedicure—the pinky polish with the white strip across the top of the nail. It literally makes me feel like a million bucks, and I notice that I act a little more pompous on my return home. Sorry, honey.

Some of my friends came out of the womb wearing a tutu and tiara. Others are still the biggest tomboys around. I'm not low-maintenance and I'm not high-maintenance, so I have dubbed that central ground as "mid-maintenance." *Justin says that only a high-maintenance person would invent a new maintenance category. But I digress.*

.........................................................................

Wear makeup because it makes you feel good.
Because it enhances the beautiful features God gave you.
Because it's fun. Don't start wearing makeup because
you think it will get you a man.

.........................................................................

God made us all unique and special. I want you to hold on to those qualities. Wear makeup because it makes you feel good. Because it enhances the beautiful features God gave you. Because it's fun.

Don't start wearing makeup because you think it will get you a man.

After enduring the awkward middle school years, my problem was not a lack of desire to be more girly, but an ignorance of the "how." My mom is the epitome of class, and she always got ready before work by putting on makeup, blow-drying her hair and keeping her perfect nails polished. I copied her routine, using the same cosmetics she did, but my results weren't as amazing. Looking back at photographs makes me realize it wasn't enough! I needed more help!

Maybe you don't wear makeup, and that's okay, but stick with me here. Facial foundation is sometimes considered part of a great skin care routine because it keeps impurities from clogging your pores. Find a foundation that matches your skin tone, and make sure it says "noncomedogenic" (non-pore-clogging) on the label. It will keep your skin safe and even out skin tone. Double bonus!

Bottom line: Makeup, skirts, and heels are tangible ways to nurture your feminine side. That's it. Allison was exactly right. Femininity is wrapped up in our DNA, whether we choose to be a cowgirl, a racecar driver, a teacher, a doctor, a housewife or an astronaut. But most important is the cultivation of a gentle and quiet spirit, for that brings forth a beauty that is irresistible.

**Notes**

1. David L. Chandler, "How Spider Webs Achieve Their Strength," Cambridge, MA: MIT-news. http://web.mit.edu/newsoffice/2012/spider-web-strength-0202.html (accessed September 27, 2012).

2. "Scientists Uncover Strength of Spider Web Design," *The Telegraph.* http://www.telegraph.co.uk/science/9056006/Scientists-uncover-strength-of-spider-web-design.html (accessed September 27, 2012).

# Availability

*I've always pursued you. I'm still pursuing you.*

JUSTIN JETT

When Reynaldo Jones saw a girl he liked, he put thought and effort into asking her out. Once, he fashioned ice into the shape of a heart and put it on the car of the girl he was crushing on. Inside the heart was a note. After a few delicate attempts to chisel the note out with her keys, she threw the ice on the ground, shattering it.

The note said, "Since you broke the ice, can I ask you out?"
*Awwwww.*
Doesn't that make your heart melt?

## Perceived Availability

I love that Reynaldo asked the girl's permission if he could ask her out. He made her feel valued with the amount of thought and care that went into his offer. He went above and beyond so that he would stand out from all the other guys vying for her attention.

Were there other guys after her? I don't know. What's important is that he thought there were, and therein lies the lesson: more important than your *actual* availability is your *perceived* availability.

Remember, this is an intentional pursuit. If a guy wants to spend time with you, he needs to put some thought into it. He doesn't have to go as far as Reynaldo's ice capade, but he needs to do more than just a "Hey, wanna go out?"[1]

I first heard about the Wednesday Rule in high school. We were in the library doing research for English class, but about four girls were talking loud enough for the entire campus to hear.

"You didn't agree to go out with him, did you?" Kacie, asked.

"Yeah, so?" said Amber.

"He waited too long to ask you." Gretchen, slid a file across her manicured nails.

Amber stared at her. "Why?"

The girl named Monica leaned forward. "Because he should have asked you out earlier. If he asked you out after Wednesday, you were probably his backup plan."

Amber put her pen down and folded her arms across her chest. "I was not his backup plan, Mon-ica," she said, glaring.

"You don't know that, Am-ber," Monica retorted. "And besides, he needs to know that he can't just call you at the last minute. If he wants to hang out with you, he needs to make sure he asks you before anyone else has a chance."

Amber made a face. "Well, I didn't have any plans."

Kacie chimed in, "It doesn't matter. You tell him that you do."

Gretchen nodded. "He'll make sure to ask you out earlier the next time."

Amber was quiet for a moment. I was quiet, too. Eavesdropping Rule #1.

"What if I say I'm busy, and then he doesn't ask me out again?"

"Then he didn't really like you in the first place, and you saved yourself some heartache."

• • • • • • • • • • • • • • • • • • • • • • • • • • • • • • • • • • • • • • • • • • • • • • • • • • •

Instead of being desperate enough to go out with anyone who would ask, these girls made guys work for them. And guys did. They had to be on to something.

• • • • • • • • • • • • • • • • • • • • • • • • • • • • • • • • • • • • • • • • • • • • • • • • • • •

I'd never thought about that. I would have said, "Jump at the chance! You only live once! YOLO." But what they said made sense. It seemed to be a nice way of guarding your heart. Instead of being desperate enough to go out with anyone who would ask, these girls made guys work for them. And guys *did*. They had to be on to something.

In a nutshell, the Wednesday Rule means if a guy doesn't ask you out for the upcoming weekend by Wednesday, you say no, even if your calendar is wide open and you've been praying for him to ask you out for the entire semester. If you say you have plans, all of a sudden you've created some mystery; and if he truly likes you, he will definitely ask you out again. If he never repeats the offer, you may have been his back-up plan.

The Wednesday Rule is really for people who don't know each other very well. If you're "talking" or "sort of together," then use the rule as a guideline. The point is to not always be available on a guy's whim.

## First Dates

First dates can be nerve-wracking. I've compiled a list of do's and don'ts so that all you'll have to worry about is what to wear. I like to start with the shoes and then build the rest of the outfit!

- Wear something dark. It'll hide any unfortunate accidents, spills, drips and the like.
- Don't eat red sauce. Save the marinara and barbeque sauce for another time.
- Order what you want to eat, not what you think will impress him.
- Bring money to cover your meal in case your date is a tightwad. If he doesn't offer to pay, don't agree to a second date.
- Let him pay.
- Drive yourself unless he's a trusted friend. You need a way to leave if things get weird and he doesn't need to know where you live.
- Don't go back to his place or invite him inside your home.
- Have a friend expecting your "I'm home" phone call. If you don't call, she's allowed to track you down.

• If you have the slightest inkling the relationship could go somewhere, get a picture. You'll thank me later.

These are first date suggestions, maybe second and third date ones too. Once you and your honey settle into a more exclusive relationship, you can start bending the rules. Justin and I ate a lot of meals together while we dated. Since we weren't married, it wasn't his responsibility to feed me! If we went on a special date, he paid, but if we ran through Mickey D's, I could buy my own and occasionally pay for his as well.

Sometimes rules are made to be broken.

I bent the Wednesday Rule with Justin.

I'd planned to eat with Justin and Bonnie on my lunch hour, and as I walked over to the apartments, I noticed Justin wearing his work uniform. "They asked me to come in early," he explained. "Can you stop by when you get off?" I agreed, disappointed to not have lunch together but eager to see him after I got off work.

I packed my belongings early so that I'd be ready to go when work ended. He'd be expecting me within a certain time parameter and I didn't want to get him in trouble at work. Thankfully, he was outside when I pulled into the parking lot.

I parked and shyly strolled over to him. He smiled his boyish grin when he spotted me. I remember wishing that everyone I knew would drive by and see me with him.

I didn't know what to say, so I just smiled and let him talk first. After the obligatory "How was your day?" and "How's work going?" he got to the point.

"I'd like to take you out sometime."

*Aaaaahhhh!!!*

"I'd like that," I said, repressing the mini-me in my brain who was doing round-off back handspring layout tucks.

"But I don't have your number."

I froze. I'd never given a guy my number before. Waves of insecurity knocked my mini-me to her feet. Was he teasing me? Did he *really* want my number, and if I gave it to him, would he call? I would feel so stupid if he didn't call me. *Be cool. Be cool.*

"Do you have something to write on?" he said.

I fished in my purse and pulled out an envelope. I wrote my number on an end of it, tore it off and handed it to him. *(That little scrap of paper is now safely tucked in a hand-painted craft box sitting on his dresser.)*

"How about tonight?" he asked. "I'm off in an hour. I would love to take you to dinner."

My heart sank as I realized tonight was the one night in 15 years that both of my parents had somewhere to be and I was babysitting my little brother. *Curses.*

"I wish I could, but I can't." I knew my face showed every ounce of the disappointment that was seeping out of my heart. He looked surprised, and I explained, "My mom is at class and my dad has a meeting tonight." I sighed. "I have to watch my little brother."

I felt like a loser as dreams of a romantic dinner crashed at my feet. Notice that I was only following the Wednesday Rule because I actually was busy. Smitten as I was, I would have said yes no matter when he asked me. So do as I say, and all that.

Justin didn't miss a beat.

"Then why don't I take both of you out to dinner?"

"Uh, ummm, well I . . ." Stammering wasn't attractive, but I wasn't thinking fast enough.

Lesson: A guy who wants you will not take no for an answer. But while letting him pay for my dinner was one thing, paying for my little brother was something else.

Sensing my hesitation, he said, "How about Dairy Queen? I'll call you as soon I get home, and we can meet at six?"

I could handle Dairy Queen. It was inexpensive, my brother would love it and it was close to home. I could have my brother tucked in bed before my parents got back. I agreed and forced myself to walk like a normal human being back to my car. Mini-me was skipping and twirling on clouds and rainbows.

I raced home. I mean, I drove safely, with my hands at ten o'clock and two o'clock, obeying every speed limit sign. As I sprinted into the house, I know I looked like a whirlwind to eight-year-old

Nathaniel, who basically caught my cell phone as I threw it at him. I leapt the stairs two at a time, shouting instructions. "We're going out to eat. I'm getting in the shower. If that phone rings, you *run* up here and get me. Do *not* answer it. Get dressed. I'll be out in a minute."

Fastest shower of my life.

I dried my hair, applied makeup, and stressed over what to wear. When I look back at our first date picture, I wonder what the heck I was thinking when I chose the light blue, long-sleeved Aeropostale top and jeans.

I looked much prettier in my head that night than the picture proves.

It was almost six o' clock, and I was ready to go. Scat Nat was dressed and getting hungry, but no phone call. Five minutes pass. Nathaniel starts whining. Another five minutes go by. I'm wondering if Justin lost my number. Maybe it was all a joke.

The longer I sat, the more furious I got at myself. *I don't wait around for boys to call me*, I thought. I buckled Nathaniel in my little coupe and drove to DQ. I'd promised him an outing, and he needed to eat. Plus, I didn't want to eat in front of Justin, so I could scarf something down before he got there. If he showed up.

He called right after we sat down with our food. His rich, velvet voice gave me tingles and imprinted in my memory banks— I still feel giddy when I think about how deep and manly he sounded.

"Hey," he said, James Dean casual. "So-and-so's car needed a jump. I'm sorry it took so long. I wanted to let you know we were on our way."

*We? WE?* I heard a girl laugh in the background.

"Oh, you're bringing a girl?" I said.

"Bonnie."

The insecurity demon eerily rose from a shallow grave in my heart, whispering doubts in my ear. "He's bringing Bonnie because he doesn't think this is a real date." "He likes her more than you." "You're a fool to think he's serious about dating you."

"Well, we're already here." I was miffed.

"Great. See you soon," he said, and hung up. I shut my flip-phone (*this was pre-iPhone, my peeps*), closed my eyes and analyzed the situation. Bonnie was my friend. Justin was a helpful guy. He wouldn't leave someone stranded. The shadow monster faded as I spoke words of truth to myself.

I realized I was actually relieved that Bonnie was coming. Now I didn't have to be the center of attention or do all the talking. There wouldn't be awkward moments of silence.

Since Nathaniel was there, it wasn't a romantic date anyway. I quickly finished my food, checked my teeth, and popped a stick of Big Red gum in my mouth.

When they arrived, Justin ordered the biggest, messiest burger on the menu, and I prepared to be humiliated when he inevitably ended up with schmear on his face and condiment drippings down his shirt. (I'm the friend who *won't* tell you there's something stuck in your teeth, because I'm selfishly embarrassed at the thought of having to inform you. Always carry a mirror if we're eating together so you can check yourself.)

That man ate the entire burger holding it in one hand, and a napkin in the other, military-style. No drips, drops, spills or anything embarrassing. I. Was. Impressed.

He bought Nathaniel some ice cream, and Bonnie graciously escorted him to the claw machine. Justin and I camped out in the booth, getting to know each other, the conversation light and easy. I didn't want the evening to end.

I subtly coerced Bonnie to take a picture of us afterwards. On the off chance that Justin and I stayed together, I wanted a tangible piece of this memory. The treasured photo is tucked inside our china cabinet and makes me smile every time I walk by.

*Always take a picture.*

The vibrations from Justin's eighties CD reverberated with every jealous beat of my heart as I watched Bonnie climb into his rugged red Jeep. I waved goodbye and backed out of the parking lot first. I wanted him to watch me leave so I wouldn't be the last one there. I went to bed replaying our conversation in my head and fell asleep with a smile on my face.

*Not.*

I overanalyzed every word out of his mouth. I called Bonnie and grilled her for half an hour to see what else he said about me. It wasn't until I'd repeated the entire evening's scenes a hundred times in my mind that I fell asleep, eager to wake up and see him again.

## Tips for Life

### Leave Him Wanting More

Always be the first one to leave. If you want to be even more memorable as you walk out the door, turn your head to address the room. The last thing you want people to see as you walk away is your pretty face, not your rear.

I purposely left the DQ parking lot before Justin. I didn't want to feel left behind (I already felt left out), and I wanted him to watch my dust kick up. Making yourself easily accessible is not in your best interests. If you're always around, it's easy for a guy to get lazy in his pursuit. The saying "familiarity breeds contempt" is true. Make him work for your attention. If you're the first one out the door, he'll use the time you have together wisely.

### Let Him Call, Text, Friend, Email or Instant Message First

This goes doubly for how you use your phone and social media. If a guy wants to talk to you, he will find a way. Our society has made it extremely easy for guys to find your picture, where you live and what you ate for breakfast by simply doing an Internet search. Haven't you already Google-stalked that guy you like? 'Cause I definitely Google-stalked Justin. Thank you, Facebook, for not being as available back then, because I would have been out of control.

Let's be real for a second. This is what typically happens when a girl likes a guy. She finds a way to exchange numbers, then she texts him. If he doesn't respond in the amount of time she's designated in her mind, she texts him again.

Girl, if that boy wanted to text you, he would have found a way to get your number, and he would have texted you back immediately. Don't keep bothering him. He either hasn't seen your text yet, or he doesn't care. A man will do what a man wants to do. Never forget that.

I once asked Justin, "If Ryan had been my boyfriend, what would you have done?" He said, "It didn't matter if you had a boyfriend. You weren't married." *Oooooh.* As cocky as he was, I loved his intensity. He knew what he wanted, and he went after it. Persistence is a sexy quality. We love when our on-screen heroes defy all odds and get the girl. It's even better when it happens in real life.

## Let Him Plan Your Next Meeting

Never suggest a second meeting. Don't even hint at it.

Justin made no mention of a second date, and I didn't offer. Our situation was a little different than most since I worked where he lived and went to school. He knew my schedule, so I said goodnight and left.

To ask a guy "When can I see you again?" implies that you are pursuing him. I take that back; it shouts desperation. Honey, he will ask you out again if he wants to. If you ask him, you can't be sure of his motivation for agreeing to a second date.

Yes, I get it; some guys are shy. I hear your objection. Perhaps he is too nervous to ask you out again. But if he's too nervous to ask to see you again, maybe he'll be too nervous to propose. Maybe he'll be too nervous to say his vows in front of a crowded room. Maybe he'll be too nervous to call the plumber after your two-year-old shoves a diaper down the toilet.

*I'm on a roll here, I can't be stopped.*

Maybe he'll be too nervous to ask for a promotion at his job. You don't want a man who is too *nervous* to go after his dreams, and if he's not dreaming of you, you need to stop dreaming of him.

This is a rule that even married gals should follow. Sometimes I must resist the urge to text my husband random flights of fancy that flow through my brain. He needs a break from the crazy, and even though I can text him whenever I want, I need to remember that I still want him to chase me. The catching is more fun now.

## God's Authority

Maneuvering the blurred roles of wife and girlfriend seem tricky, but thankfully, we have a God who laid it out for us. God gave us three commands when it comes to the men in our lives. "Honor your father" (Eph. 6:2), "respect [your] husband" (Eph. 5:33), and "submit to your husband as to the Lord" (vv. 22-24).

God never mentions your betrothed. The rules that apply to your future spouse *do not* apply in your dating life. This is especially important when we talk about the dreaded "S" word. When you're dating, you are not required to "submit" to your boyfriend. Don't do it.

Do you see? God thinks so much of us—He treasures us so immensely—that He keeps us under the protection of *two* men. When I turned 16, my daddy told me, "The Bible doesn't say you can stop honoring me when you turn 18." I guess he wanted those words to sink in for a couple of years.

At our wedding, when my preacher said the words, "Who gives this woman to this man?" my father squeezed my hand and said, "Her mother and I do." He lifted my veil, kissed my cheek and placed my right hand into Justin's outstretched one. Forever.

My daddy relinquished his God-ordained position as my "head" and put me under the "authority" of Justin. What a treasured moment!

Don't get profeminist-Nazi on me here. I understand that not all girls are able, or even want, their fathers to give them away at their wedding. What a beautiful thing it is to see an uncle (or two!), a brother, a mother, a grandparent or a stepfather escort a bride down the aisle. The significance is the "giving away" and publicly "releasing" the beloved little girl to a man who promises to take care of her and love her for the rest of her days.

Submitting to your boyfriend is not practice for when you get married. You are not bound by any God-ordained means to submit. And since our culture spits that word when it says it, let's give the word crystal-clear meaning.

Here's your hierarchy pre-marriage: God. Parents. You.

After marriage: Christ. Husband. You (see Eph. 5:25-33).

This does not make you inferior, and anyone who tells you different is wrong.

You don't get your driver's license without reading the handbook, and honey, you shouldn't get your wedding license until you've read God's manual. Society has perverted what marriage was intended to be. By following God's system, there's less room for heartache. He didn't create the rules to hurt us.

> You don't get your driver's license without reading the handbook, and honey, you shouldn't get your wedding license until you've read God's manual.

Your husband has more on the line than you do. Just as Christ is the head of the Church, the husband is the head of the household. This doesn't mean he gets to boss you around. It doesn't mean you are a walking doormat. It doesn't mean you lose your identity. I have so much to say on submission, but since we're not submitting to our boyfriends, *or fiancés*, we'll save that conversation for another time.

A marriage is a partnership. You're a team. So while you're dating, you need to make sure that you trust that boy to listen to God when it comes to every decision. Because when you're married, and he says, "I think God wants me to take this job 500,000 miles away from our friends and family," you're gonna be faced with a choice. If you don't trust him to be in daily communion with God, then don't you dare agree to marry him.

Your availability to your boyfriend is not exclusive amounts of time. Don't move in together before you're married. If you're already living together, move out. I don't care that it's going to cost tons of money or that you can't afford it. Get married or get out. Do you think God can or will bless disobedience?

Spending unlimited amounts of time with your honey is a marriage perk. Until that boy slides a wedding ring on your finger, unlimited access denied.

What does that look like? When we were dating, I didn't *have* to answer Justin's phone calls. I didn't *have* to explain where I spent my money. I didn't *have* to do everything with him, because we weren't married. I don't *have* to do those things now, but the accountability level has changed, and as my husband, partner and teammate, he gets more access. Every activity, phone call, date was a choice and a privilege. I loved being with him, and I chose to share aspects of my life with him, but he wasn't entitled to it.

## One Foot Out the Door

If a man takes you for granted, you have a choice: set him straight or become his doormat. And by set him straight, I mean tell him to cut it out or you're walking.

Run if you have to.

Dating can be romantic and wonderful and flowers and *controlled* passion—but while your head is in the clouds, be sure to keep one foot firmly planted on the ground. You might have to turn and run.

I read that a person can be on his or her best behavior for about six months. After that time frame, his or her true colors show through. I broke up with Justin after eight months.

When we started dating, we made a commitment that if, at any time, one of us couldn't see ourselves getting married, we'd break up. This talk came early on and I know it helped take the pressure off, for me anyway. I had given myself an "out" up front, and we knew that every day we were together was because we had the end goal of forever in front of us.

The day came when I thought he was going to break up with me. I felt like he was taking for granted the time I spent with him. I thought I liked him more than he liked me. I couldn't bear for him to dump me, so I beat him to the punch.

On the way home from the mall one day, I worked up the courage to tell him what I was thinking. Instead of hinting, I spelled it out. "I think you take me for granted."

We were getting off the highway and were in the 25-MPH-loop around. He turned his head and looked at me. "What are you talking about?"

I took a deep breath and stated my reasons. He nodded his head and kept driving.

That's when I knew. He didn't care about me as much as I liked him. I loved him, but I wasn't going to be last place in his life while he waited for someone better to come along and have him dump me. I had to be in control of the breakup because his breaking up with me would be devastating.

A good friend will tell you the truth, even when it's hard to hear. Windy was dating (and later married) my Justin's roommate and best friend, Justin. *It's true.*

Windy told me she'd never seen my Justin so miserable. "He sat in chapel with his head down the whole time. He's walking around in a daze." She lowered her voice. "My Justin said he heard your Justin crying in his room the other night." Then her voice returned to a normal volume. "What are you doing to him? He's in love with you."

*My Justin* cried over me? *My Justin* is walking around in a daze? From the bottom of my heart, I thought he'd be fine. I didn't expect him to be very affected by our breakup. Windy knew I hated being apart from him, and thankfully she brought to my attention that I needed to rethink my decision. While trying to protect my heart, I hurt his.

Not sure what to do, I called my grandma.

"I broke up with your grandpa once," she said.

*What?!?!*

My grandparents had a love I dreamed about.

"Sometimes it takes a good breakup for a boy to know what he has," she continued. "I've seen the way Justin looks at you. You two will be okay."

I love my grandma.

It's funny how that's all I remember of the breakup—talking to Windy and getting comfort from my grandma. I don't remember how Justin and I got back together, and neither does he. It's like we erased that painful memory. I know it happened, but thankfully my brain didn't retain it.

I don't regret that breakup, but let me be clear that I did not break up with him to teach him a lesson. Sometimes a little bit of space is a good thing. Dating is hard, fun, stressful and exciting. The more work you put in to your dating relationship, the better (easier?) marriage can be.

My friend Katy had a similar experience, except instead of giving her too much space, her boyfriend was smothering her. She wasn't sure if she was ready for marriage, and he was already planning the venue.

## Katy's Story

Jake and I had been dating for almost a year when I broke up with him. I was scared that I was getting too comfortable and could no longer make decisions for myself.

If our relationship was becoming unhealthy with the amount of time we were spending together and the speed of seriousness, I needed to know I could still leave. I prayed about it, but I didn't allow God to give me peace. So I ended the relationship out of fear. I didn't want to marry someone like my dad, so I broke up with Jake. I needed to do it. For me.

For the week we were broken up, Jake never stopped fighting for me. He never stopped being there when I needed him. He was trying to guard his heart, so he didn't tell me he loved me, didn't compliment me, but he kept pursuing. He gave me the space I needed and the time to pray and consider our future together.

We got back together. Jake is forgiving and gracious. He told me that he knew we wouldn't be breaking up forever; he knew that I needed to do this even though it hurt. It made me realize that he really loves me. Unconditionally loves me. Jake is nothing like my dad. He is kind, gracious, forgiving, loving, Christ centered, compassionate, passionate about people, doesn't give up and he encourages me in Christ. He knows my heart and makes every effort to guard it. He protects me.

## Keep Your Friends Available

Some relationships skip the friendship phase, like my relationship with Justin. Others are built on years of friendship, like David and Mallory's.

They had been friends since grade school, had mutual friends and attended the same church. Their dads were both sponsors in the youth group. When I was in high school, they were young middle schoolers; but in high school, David wanted something more. He asked Mallory to a movie on a double date (nice move—nonthreatening) and after the movie, he popped the question. "So, are we . . . together . . ?"

Mallory's response? An exuberant "Sure!"

What's most impressive about David and Mallory is their ability to lead separate but together lives. Mallory continued with her career path, participated in sports, remained close to her family and had regular girl nights with her friends. David did likewise. They supported each other while keeping their friends as major players in their lives.

> A telltale sign of an unhealthy relationship, perhaps a codependent one, is when a couple starts dating and stops investing in other relationships.

"Friendships are so important when you're dating someone; and if you think about it, most of those friendships were there long before your relationship," Mallory said. "We found it important to have time with each other, as well as time with our friends. We were lucky to share a good number of mutual friends. That made it easy since everyone already was used to spending time together."

It's so easy, too easy, to alienate people once you become serious with someone. A telltale sign of an unhealthy relationship, perhaps a codependent one, is when a couple starts dating and stops investing in other relationships.[2] While you *looove* your boyfriend and always want to be near him because you can't get enough of him, grow up! There has to be some balance.

I'm all for spending time with your boyfriend. Being a consistent part of each other's lives is important and shouldn't feel like a chore. It's fun if you share similar interests, but it's just as fun to teach someone else how to do something you love.

You are special.

You are worth having a guy work to gain your attention.

Choose carefully whom you allow into your private sphere. When the love of your life loves you more than life, honey, hang on and enjoy being the center of his world.

**Notes**

1. The Ice Capades was a traveling entertainment show featuring theatrical performances involving ice skating (see http://en.wikipedia.org/wiki/Ice_Capades). I'm not talking about the performance, just a play on words. You understand. ☺
2. According to the PsychCentral website, "Co-dependency occurs when two people form a relationship with each other because neither feels that he or she can 'stand alone.'" See "Co-dependent Relationships," PsychCentral, http://psychcentral.com/library/id63.html

# 8

# Communication

*Flirting is the art of keeping intimacy at a safe distance.*

SABRINA SESSELMANN

If a boy is mean to a girl, chances are good he has a crush on her. In the book *Anne of Green Gables*, Gilbert Blythe dunks Anne's hair into an inkwell and pulls her red braids while name-calling, "Carrots!" She hates him. He loves her.

Science shows that boys' brains and girls' brains develop in different sequences. "These researchers concluded that the areas of the brain involved in language, in spatial memory, in motor coordination, and in getting along with other people, develop in a 'different order, time, and rate' in girls compared with boys."[1]

Boys have great motor coordination at an earlier age, while girls are able to communicate earlier. It's not the boy's fault—his brain hasn't developed that area yet. When we take the reins and spout off our romantic notions and declarations of love, we try to reap what we've sown, but that seed isn't falling on fertile ground yet (see Matt. 13:1-23). We need to give the guys a little grace and let them catch up.

## Allison's Story: Boy Fast

Our reputations are fragile, and a bad rep is hard to overcome. God warns us to avoid all appearance of evil (see 1 Thess. 5:22), which means we need to be mindful of how we're acting, pretty much at all times—especially with guys. Allison learned this the hard way.

> Someone at my small private Christian college started a nasty rumor about me. They said I had "hit it and quit it" with a guy I was really good friends with. It was embarrassing and humiliating. Luckily, all my friends knew that I am a virgin and stopped that rumor before it got too crazy.
>
> I cried for a couple of hours at my mentor's house. I didn't want rumors like that to even be a thought in someone's mind. My mentor encouraged me to go on a "boy fast." It was different than anything I'd ever heard of. I could still be friends with boys, but texting them was not allowed (unless it was about homework), and hanging out with them one-on-one was not encouraged.
>
> We talked about what flirting looked like. The posture I stood in, what I did with my hands, if I played with my hair, whether I smiled over silly things, etc. She had me tally my flirting. (This is what helped a lot.)
>
> On my left hand, I marked every time I caught myself flirting, and on my right hand I marked every time I stopped myself.
>
> Day One was super sad. I was really disappointed with myself, but the honesty felt good. Over time, my right hand was marked so much more than my left, and that made me want to stop flirting altogether. It was like a competition with myself.
>
> I did this "boy fast" for an entire year.
>
> It was actually really hard on my heart. I was used to getting my validation from guys, from flirting and feeling desired by them. There were nights I cried out to God, asking Him to fill me up and to make me complete in Him. I needed to find my value in God and my worth in His Word.

If flirting is an issue, you don't have to go to the extreme of marking your hands, but figure out a way to become aware. Flirting with a guy you aren't interested in is not fair to him. He's a brother in Christ, and his feelings are important. They matter. It's not fair for him to get his hopes up if there is not a chance in this world you would date him. He could be looking for Mrs. Right while you play with his heart.

...................................................................

Flirting with a guy you aren't interested in is not fair to him. He's a brother in Christ, and his feelings are important.

...................................................................

Similarly, some girl could be flirting with your future guy, even though she's not interested. Don't you want her to leave your man alone? Then do the same for the other women waiting.

Flirting with the guy you like is a lot of fun, provided it's done right. Some of our flirting is subconscious. Our bodies release pheromones, which are hormones that cause attraction. When a girl flips or plays with her hair while talking to a cute boy, she's releasing those sex-attractant hormones! You can even purchase pheromones in roll-on and spray forms. My friend who sells the product says she's had waitress customers who wear it before shifts because they swear they get better tips.

## Prayer

While extra pheromones might help get your guy to notice you, prayer is the most valuable weapon in your arsenal. Pray for your future husband. Pray for yourself. Pray that you'll treat each other respectfully. Pray that you tumble head-over-heels in love. God knows the desire of your heart, and if you want to have a passion-ate fireworks-kind-of-love, then ask Him for it.

When Justin and I were in the "talking" stage, I was praying my heart out. I needed the spiritual "go-ahead" before I took the step and accepted his invitation to be his girlfriend. I didn't want to make a mistake. I didn't want to waste our time.

Praying for your future spouse is critical. Don't you hope he's praying for you?

Allison shares her story about praying for Matthew:

One day out of the blue, I started desiring a relationship. I went off alone and prayed for hours. I asked God to help me be okay with never being in a relationship, that no one would replace the incredible relationship I'd built with Him.

I read somewhere that you should spend as much time with Jesus as you would with a boyfriend—this mindset was incredible. I would find myself daydreaming about the next time I could go off by myself and pray and read and spend time with my man (Jesus).

After about a year, the same time I desired a relationship, my friend Matthew and I began hanging out more and more. I prayed that I wouldn't flirt with him, that we would remain friends and that our hearts would be guarded. We didn't spend time alone and were in groups all the time. One day we were hanging out and he asked to talk to me alone. He told me that he liked me a lot and would like to take me on a date.

I asked him if he'd prayed about it and he said he'd been praying about it for two weeks. I told him that I wanted two weeks to pray about it too. During that time, I think we hung out alone once. We still guarded our hearts. After two weeks of lots of prayer, I felt peace. I felt God's blessing on a relationship with Matthew. I told him that I liked him, too, and I accepted his date offer. We went on a helicopter ride, and dating him has been one of the greatest blessings in my life.

## When to Say "I Love You"

The thing with guys is that they will accept almost any female invitation offered. They're hormonal and are usually idiots when it comes to girls. Let's face it, most men have a "sure, why not?" mentality. Thus, if a girl is decently attractive, most guys are willing to go out. The only way a girl can be certain that a guy wants to date *her* is to let him ask. This is why I didn't pursue Justin in any manner. And it was delightful! I knew he wanted to spend time with me.

Same principle applies for saying the "L" word. Mallory let David say it first. They had been dating for about a month. He went to her house the evening before his high school basketball tryouts. She walked him to his car and surprised him with a "good-luck" box she'd filled with all kinds of goodies and notes. She says, "David seemed so appreciative—he just took the box, stared at me and then told me he loved me. I was so shocked I didn't even say it back right away."

············································································

When he asked me to marry him, I knew it was
because he didn't want to let me go.

············································································

Justin said "I love you" first, and I knew he meant it. Had I said it first, I would always have wondered if he said it back out of politeness, natural response or because he actually knew that he did. The same goes for proposals. When he asked me to marry him, I knew it was because he didn't want to let me go.

## Appreciation

Justin and I had our first date on Valentine's Day (unintentionally), and became a couple on February 17. We were sitting in the Student Union Building in a love seat. His arm was draped casually across the top, and I loved sitting so close to him. Bonnie had warned him that I was still in my "purposeful singleness" stage and wasn't sure if I was ready to date him.

*Bonnie, I love you for telling him that. You are such an amazing friend, always looking to protect the hearts of people you love.*

We'd been "talking" for a few weeks and I was falling fast for him. He nonchalantly said, "I really want you to go out with me."

"I wouldn't be sitting here if I didn't want to," I replied.

We sat in satisfied silence until some guys ran through the building, whooping and hollering. I like to think they were unknowingly celebrating our milestone.

Like I said, we had our first date on Valentine's Day, February 14. Get this: we officially started dating February 17. Justin's birthday is February 18.

*Really?*

I felt like the guy who asks a girl out on February 13 and is then committed to Valentine's Day hoopla for a girl he's been dating less than 24 hours.

Had I not agreed to be his girlfriend, I would have wished him a happy birthday and perhaps written him a birthday note. Now I was his girlfriend, and all I could think of was stories urging girls to not buy their guys expensive presents. Let him spend his money on you—you're the present. But I felt the need to get him something. I went to Blockbuster and picked up a $10 gift card and tucked it inside a greeting card. When he came into my office after one of his classes, I wished him a happy birthday and handed him the envelope.

He looked at me in disbelief, took it from me and stared at it for a second. I thought maybe he thought it was booby-trapped the way he held it so gingerly. I smiled encouragingly and he ripped the envelope down the short side instead of the normal way, tipped it and let the card slide into his hand.

He obligingly read the front and his eyes grew wide when he saw the gift card. His appreciative smile is seared in my memory. He hadn't expected a gift, and his thorough enjoyment of receiving a present made me determine to make every birthday I spent with him a wonderful one. And I have.

When you're dating someone in a committed relationship, you have freedom to enjoy each other's interest, and you should let the person know how you feel about him. As women, we have to make sure we're not the ones bestowing the most affection. Although it comes easier to us, we need to give him room to step up.

On our next Valentine's Day, the one-year anniversary of our first date, and two days before our official "one-year-together" status, Justin took me to Dairy Queen to celebrate where it all started. If we took a picture, I can't find it.

When we arrived back at the college, he pulled into the parking area by the dorms but didn't park in a lined space. Instead, he pulled up onto where the grass met the asphalt and turned off the engine.

"What are you doing?" I asked. I was afraid a Resident Assistant (RA) would come over and tell us to move, or worse yet, have my boss be on campus for some reason and see us. While I avoid confrontation, Justin faces it head-on. He wasn't worried a bit.

"Open your door for some air," he said. "And turn around. I have a surprise."

I squealed and promptly turned around.

For what felt like was forever. For-ev-er.

When I heard him open and shut the trunk and start fiddling with wires and cords, I started to get annoyed. Was he tinkering with an electronic device? I rested my shoulder against the seat and leaned my head on the headrest.

Finally, he walked around to my open door and took my hand. "Close your eyes," he said, and led me around the car. I felt the ground soften as we stepped onto the grass from the pavement. He pulled my hand and told me to sit. I obeyed, and felt the softness of a blanket instead of the expected scratchy grass.

"Can I open them?" I asked. I could hardly keep from peeking but didn't want to ruin the delicious surprise.

"Hold on," he said from somewhere behind me. After a second, he joined me on the blanket. "Now," he said.

I opened my eyes and gasped. In front of us, huge as life, was a picture of the two of us projected on the two-story dorm building. The song "Angel Eyes" by The Jeff Healey Band started playing from his laptop, and for the next three-and-a-half minutes, a slideshow of our first year together flashed on the building for all to see.

Some of the other students arriving home stopped and watched from a distance so they wouldn't interrupt our private moment.

Best. Present. Ever.

## When to Share Your Secrets

We all have these moments of self-preservation, moments when we stop like a deer that hears footsteps in an otherwise quiet meadow. We sense danger, but we can't see which direction it's coming from. We feel the red laser pointed at our chest but can't see the point of origin.

So we freeze. We listen. We are still. With bated breath, we crouch inside our hearts, pick up a brick and place it in front of us. Still listening to the silence, we pick up another and lay it next to the first. With each moment, we pick up a brick, naming it as we build our walls.

*Rejection. Disappointment.*

Sometimes we call the bricks by other names.

*Worthless. Forgotten. Excluded.*

We slather the mortar of fear across each section, rarely allowing it to set before more bricks are placed on top.

*Ugly. Stupid. Naughty.*

We build walls around our hearts to protect ourselves so we can't get hurt too deeply.

We prepare for warnings.

Before I started dating Justin, a coworker who had been a youth sponsor at Justin's church cautioned me that I needed to be careful—that Justin had some serious baggage. My friend Ryan warned me to guard my heart; and another friend who'd been in a small group with Justin told me the same thing.

It sounds crazy to ignore warnings, but in my soul I was confident that unless he'd killed or raped someone, I could handle whatever information in his past was causing people who cared about me such concern. The hypocrite in me, however, knows that if my sister had a crush on someone, and I knew about these warnings, I would have jumped on the cautionary bandwagon as well and advised her against dating the guy.

Though Justin grew up going to church, the lifestyle he led while in the military was in direct opposition to his upbringing. In November of 2001, his life hit rock bottom after attending a party and making a horrible decision.

We'd been dating for about two months when Justin confessed his past. We were about to get in the Jeep, but instead of climbing in the seat, he stood with his hand on the hood and a sad look on his face.

He knew I'd been warned that he came with baggage, and in an effort to beat any well-intentioned do-gooder to the punch, he knew he had to tell me.

So he spilled his guts. As he talked, I thought about that night when I felt God's peace regarding my future husband's sexual past. God had prepared my heart for this moment. My love for Justin grew as every shameful act caused his head to droop and his voice grew softer and softer. Each word was painful for him; and while I listened quietly, my heart cried out for God to wrap His arms of peace around Justin. After he finished, his head almost completely bowed, he glanced at me from lowered lids and asked for my forgiveness.

I picture every repentant word out of his mouth cracking the foundation of the walls he had set up. Trust destroyed the Fear mortar he'd thickly applied. Love smashed each hurtful name he'd called himself. Forgiveness destroyed every label.

Ten years later, as we sit in our family room, I ask him about that night.

"I realized my life was way off track," he said. "I started listening to Christian talk radio on my drive to and from work. I feel like I must have been extremely far from God that I was able to even do what I did," he said. "I cried a lot on my drives. There are certain things you can never undo. I would think, *What have I done?* So I turned my life around, applied to Bible college and met you."

"Were you scared to tell me about your past?" I ask. "We talked about it pretty early on in our dating life."

"I was kind of nervous. I didn't know exactly what you'd think."

"How did you feel after you told me and I wasn't repulsed by you?" I put my hand on his arm. *I'm distracting him with my questions and I want to hear his answers.*

"Like I'd held my breath for an hour waiting for your response."

"And then?" I prompted.

He took a deep breath. "I was extremely relieved, but at the same time I was thinking, *She's not gonna stay . . . like this is not gonna last.* I thought you'd go, 'I like him, but that's too much. I'm not doing that.'"

There wasn't much that he could have said that night to scare me away. Maybe murder. Maybe if he was a father. But not for the repentant heart that trusted me with his secrets.

......................................................................................

No matter what's hiding in your past, you don't have
to confess to everyone. You can't take words back.

......................................................................................

Never think that you have to share your secrets just because someone told you theirs. Like it or not, there's still a double standard when it comes to the sexual experiences of boys and girls. No matter what's hiding in your past, you don't have to confess to everyone. You can't take words back.

I did not offer my story to Justin that night. It was soon enough for him to tell me, but too early for me to tell him. I hadn't told *anyone* that I wasn't perfect. After repenting of it a couple of years earlier, I'd promised God and myself that the only person I needed to tell was my future husband. And if things didn't work out with Justin, then that promise would have been broken. I kept it to myself until I felt that Justin could be completely trusted with my heart.

Justin needed to get his past off his chest early in our relationship. He felt pressure from people who wanted to "warn me," so he wanted me to hear about his past from him and not someone else. I respected him for it. I still do.

If you're hiding a dirty little secret and feel the need to blab, tell God. Write it down in the privacy of your journal. Confide in a close friend or mentor. Don't tell any guy until you're convinced he's ready to handle it. Guard your heart until God brings you the man who can forgive and forget.

## Sexting

If you had to hand your phone to a friend or parent, how many texts would you want to delete first? It's a wonder the 1-900-dial-a-slut companies aren't out of business, since most guys can get the same pleasure from texting their girlfriends. Sext—sex by text.

Why send dirty messages? Why send racy pictures?

Admit it. We like to know we've turned our man on. Knowing that we have the sexual prowess makes us feel like Cleopatra. Plus, sending sexts, images or video feels safer because no one else is in the room. We can imagine ourselves doing whatever we want, with no ridicule.

- - - - - - - - - - - - - - - - - - - - - - - - - - - - - - - - - - - - - - - - - - - - - - - - - - - - - -

We don't always realize that the sexiest thing
we can do is make our man wait.

- - - - - - - - - - - - - - - - - - - - - - - - - - - - - - - - - - - - - - - - - - - - - - - - - - - - - -

Unfortunately, we don't always realize that the sexiest thing we can do is make our man wait. It's human nature to want what you can't have, and if he can't have you, how much harder do you think he's going to pursue?

Don't say, "If I don't do it, some other girl will." If he's willing to find another girl to satisfy his needs, you've lucked out. He showed you his dirtbag-ery early on. Next!

Want to know something scary? Forty-eight percent of teens say they have received sexually suggestive messages via text, email or IM. Thirty-nine percent have sent or posted them.[2] Some of those teenagers are underage; thus, taking and sending naked photos constitutes child pornography.

Justin and I were counselors at a Christian summer camp a few months ago, and we were strictly informed during the staff meeting that under no circumstances were we to have our cell phones out or left unattended. The media director told a story about a male counselor who got arrested for child pornography when one of his campers took a naked picture of himself as a joke when the counselor left his phone on his bunk.

What does it say about our society when nakedness is no longer private? Honey, under no circumstance should you send any type of provocative picture to your boyfriend. Heaven forbid you send it to your grandparents by accident. Not only is it trashy, but how are you going to get that photo back in the event that you break up? How will you prevent him from passing it on to his friends?

Don't tell me "He's not like that." You'd be surprised what a person is capable of when pushed to the limit. If you don't take provocative photos, you don't ever have to worry about seeing yourself posted on the Internet. Those files cannot be retrieved once they're out in the Interweb. (*Ah, the word "Interweb" always makes me laugh.*)

With our world as sex-crazed as it is, I know it can be tempting to flaunt what you've got. Resist the urge to compete with scantily clad images and desperate girls willing to show more skin.

A man needs to commit to your heart before you commit with your body. You're holding out for something better.

Your husband's eyes are the only eyes worthy of taking in your full beauty.

Purity paves the way to intimacy. Purity paves the way to no regrets.

**Notes**

1. "Are There Actually Significant Differences Between a Girl's Brain and a Boy's Brain?" National Association for Single Sex Public Education (NASSPE), as quoted from Harriet Hanlon, Robert Thatcher and Marvin Cline, "Gender Differences in the Development of EEG Coherence in Normal Children," *Developmental Neuropsychology,* 1999, vol. 16, no. 3, p. 502. http://www.singlesexschools.org/research-brain.htm (accessed October 19, 2012). "Similar results were reported in a smaller study by A. P. Anokhin and associates: Complexity of Electrocortical Dynamics in Children: Developmental Aspects," *Developmental Psychobiology,* 2000, no. 36, pp. 9-22.
2. "Sex and Tech: Results from a Survey of Teens and Young Adults," The National Campaign to Prevent Teen and Unplanned Pregnancy (accessed February 27, 2013). http://www.thenationalcampaign.org/sextech/pdf/sextech_summary.pdf.

# 9

## *Boundaries*

*Boundaries are to protect life, not to limit pleasures.*

EDWIN LOUIS COLE

Justin never asked me to have sex while we were dating, but one night I pressured him. It was totally out of my character, but sometimes sin gets the better of you.

We'd been dating for almost two years and had been engaged for three months. Working on Valentine's Day was not fun, since I'd been on my feet all day at a retail clothing store where shoppers rushed in for last-minute presents. The product from the lingerie displays, which had been set up for weeks in anticipation of high sales, was going out of the store like crazy.

With each purchase, my jealousy rose, and temptation plagued me the entire evening.

*I'm tired of being the good girl.*

*It's our two-year anniversary.*

*I'm sick of doing the right thing all the time.*

*I'm 21 years old. Sex isn't a big deal.*

*We're getting married in a few months anyway.*

I used my awesome store discount and bought a black lace cami-and-panty set. Since Justin worked across the street from the mall, and we got off at the same time, he was my ride home. When I got in the car, I showed him my purchase. His forehead creased and his eyebrows furrowed together. I started my pitch with "It's our anniversary . . . yada yada yada . . . let's find a hotel." I fluttered my lashes, hoping he'd be turned on by my sudden bad-girl mojo.

He said no.

*Ehrrr?*

*This* is the kind of man I want you to find! *This* is the kind of man I urge you to wait for. This is what it means to date a guy who is spiritually stronger than you.

It had been almost two years of dating . . . of waiting . . . and wanting . . . and he said no.

I felt frustrated and embarrassed at his rejection, but he didn't make me feel stupid about it. He held my hand and sweetly, gently, reminded me I was worth waiting for.

........................................................................................

We'd set boundaries early in our relationship. I made it clear that I was waiting until my wedding night to have sex; but the more serious I got with Justin the less I relied on God.

........................................................................................

We'd set boundaries early in our relationship. I made it clear that I was waiting until my wedding night to have sex; but the more serious I got with Justin the less I relied on God. My mediocre prayer life and virtually nonexistent Bible reading gave Satan a foothold (see Eph. 4:27).

Thankfully, Justin resisted. He said he felt no hesitation, no second thought. He loved me and wanted to wait.

## Setting a Boundary

As a high school student, I facilitated abstinence education through a group called RESPECT. We taught six boundaries:

Friendly Look and Smiles
Hold Hands
Put Arms Around
Hold Close and Kiss
Further Physical Contact
Have Sex

We subconsciously set these boundaries in every relationship. The boundary with your parents is different than the boundary with teachers, coworkers, friends or siblings. These boundaries are rarely verbalized because that would just be weird. Imagine telling your friend, "I think our boundary should be putting our arms around each other."

Get away from me, weirdo.

What if you walked up to your boss and said, "Holding hands would be inappropriate, so I'm drawing our boundary line at friendly looks and smiles." You might get fired for sexual harassment.

Since boundaries are understood by position and social status, we don't bring them up in our dating life. We use television, our friends and our parents to determine what is appropriate instead of talking about it.

But here's the thing: If you can't talk about it, you definitely shouldn't be doing it.

The problem comes when we think our opinion is law. It doesn't matter what *we* think about premarital sex—the issue is what God says.

He says, "Abstain from . . . sexual immorality. You will do well to avoid these things" (Acts 15:29).

Remember, we're talking about being pursued by a man who wants you. He is not interested in being "friends-only," and most guys will gladly take all the physical goodness they can get. A man in pursuit wants your body, but a man in pursuit *who loves you* values your soul.

## Boundaries with Words

When you lose part of yourself, it's amazing what you will let people get away with.

Even though we were dating, Derek really liked this girl in our classes. I didn't think he stood a chance with her, which is a dumb thing to think, since he was dating me. I'm confident he would have dumped me for her. So why wasn't I confident enough to walk away? Just thinking about it makes me want to throw my hands in the air and shake my fist at my 15-year-old self. What does Taylor Swift say? "When you're 15 and somebody tells you they love you, you're gonna believe them."[1]

It's true.

But we really thought we loved each other. And we did. Just not the right kind of love. Sometimes we fought like brother and sister. Sometimes we acted like friends.

When it came to this girl, I was good enough for him but she was out of his league. We were all in the same classes. In our dance period, he kept sitting by her, trying to be her partner. When my feelings got hurt, he called me the "B" word.

"[Love] is not rude" (1 Cor. 13:4-5).

I'd never been called that before, but I accepted it and felt myself feeling smaller every day. Fighting was normal for our relationship. It was just who we were.

That's the second lie I told myself.

The truth is that love is not easily angered (see 1 Cor. 13:5).

I wanted to break up "for real" in the middle of our senior year, but prom was coming up, and we either had to buy tickets or not go. Missing our senior prom wasn't an option, and it was too late to find another date, so we stayed together. We wanted to break up after prom but stayed together so we wouldn't face the big world of college alone.

Fear is a horrible reason to remain in a relationship.

The first week of college held several activities for the freshman class, most of them unofficial welcomes from the local bars and clubs. Derek went with his roommate to a wet T-shirt contest at a bar, had a few drinks and watched a girl from our high school win the competition.

I was done.

For the next few hours, I sat by myself in the lounge area of the dorm, feeling angry and indignant, ignoring the happy people playing pool a few yards away. I didn't know anyone else on campus, and my roommate was a self-proclaimed beast of a girl from New Jersey who was enjoying the partying life. I had nowhere to go and no one to talk to.

So I got back together with Derek instead of leaning on God. God wasn't tangible, so I chose the seen for the unseen, the temporary for the eternal (see 2 Cor. 4:18).

It can be hard to pinpoint emotional abuse. Couples are going to fight, so what separates an argument from something worse?

In premarital counseling, Justin and I learned the rules of "fighting fair:"

Don't call names.

Don't bring up the past.

Never let a man talk down to you. His words should be sweet like honey. If you're constantly feeling "not good enough" because of how he treats you, you should ask a friend what he or she thinks about your relationship. Friends are always willing to share an opinion.

## Boundaries with Stuff

Dating a guy does not give him access to your money or your home. Keep that guy out of your bank account(s) until he's willing to give you his last name. I waited until after my name was legally changed before dealing with banking paperwork.

Your home is your refuge. Moving in with a guy to see if you're compatible is ridiculous. The first year of marriage is so great because you're learning to live together. When you're dating, he doesn't get to leave a toothbrush in your bathroom, and he doesn't get a drawer. If he wants to save money on rent, he can get a roommate until he's ready to make a commitment to you.

We've all heard the saying, "Why buy the cow when you can get the milk for free"? In other words, why would a guy obligate his life to a woman if she's already having sex with him?

Justin's military buddy Mike was living the good life. He shared his apartment with his girlfriend and their child. He'd recently earned a promotion. His life was pretty solid, except his girlfriend was constantly dropping hints about getting married, leaving engagement ring photos in magazines lying around. He was getting fed up with the constant wedding talk, but I didn't blame her.

They'd played house for a few years, and she was ready to make their family official.

For Mike, since they were already living together, sharing bank accounts and had a kid together, why did he need "a piece of paper" to show he loved her? Her thoughts were, *What is he waiting for? Why wouldn't he marry me?*

Simple. He didn't have to.

He was already living the life. To him, marriage was just a legal document for what they were already doing. To Krista, marriage meant a lifelong commitment.

What would their life together have looked like if they'd gotten married before moving in together? Before having sex? Before starting a family?

Because she gave in, from whatever internal pressure she was feeling, and moved in with Mike, she wasn't chased. As a result, she felt frustrated. Part of her soul, the part that God created to be nurtured and pursued, longed for Mike to want her. Feelings of insecurity, uncertainty and timidity about who she was as a woman popped up when he dragged his feet to propose.

She got fed up and left, taking their daughter with her, and Mike was left with two gaping holes in his heart.

## Sticking to Your Boundary

King Henry VIII of England is infamously known for his many wives. His second wife, Anne Boleyn, was a lady of the court when he met her. Legend has it that she refused to be his mistress, demanding her honor be respected. Henry became obsessed with her. He pursued her with the full force of his crown, making enemies out of allies and risking disapproval of the Pope. He annulled his marriage with a true princess and took Anne to be his queen.

She was not crowned because of true love or her personality. Anne Boleyn became Queen of England because she upheld her boundary.

It's wise to set a strict boundary, because wherever you draw the line, it will get tested. If your boundary stops at holding hands, the next thing a guy will try is to put his arm around you. If your boundary is to hold close and kiss, the next step is further physical contact.

........................................................................

It's wise to set a strict boundary, because wherever you draw the line, it will get tested.

........................................................................

I encourage you to steer clear of anything beyond kissing. Once you delve into the realm of Further Physical Contact, it can be hard to pull back. With each advance into a boundary category, it becomes easier to start there. If you kiss every guy you date, holding hands isn't a big deal. When kissing becomes commonplace, you will look to the next boundary line for excitement. And that's where you start getting into trouble.

The beautiful thing about Jesus is that He forgives us when we mess up. Whether you've started touching inappropriately or had sex, if you confess your sins, He is faithful and just and will forgive your sins and purify you from all unrighteousness (see 1 John 1:9). Even if you're currently in a sexual relationship, you don't have to continue. You can reset a boundary at any time.

Want to test the strength of your relationship? My challenge: Stop fooling around. Don't do anything beyond a kiss hello, a hug goodbye. What will happen if your time together is spent talking, playing a card game or donating time to a service project? See how long your relationship lasts when sex is off the table.

A man who truly loves you does not need to have sex with you. First of all, he hasn't earned it. Look at your left hand. Is there a wedding band there? No? Then set a boundary!

## Boundary Tips

Physical attraction is an essential element in dating, and when your guy is a major cutie, you want to hold his hand, have him put his arm around you, snuggle and be held so tight you capture the scent of him after you pull away. I get it.

Come close, I want to repeat our secret.

The more he wants you, the harder he's going to pursue you. Here are some ways to stay true to your boundary and not feel like a prude.

If your boundary is Holding Hands, mix it up a little. Trace words in his palm and have him guess what you're spelling. Rub your thumb along his. Intertwine your fingers. Give him a hand massage. It doesn't have to be boring!

For those of you at the boundary of Put Arms Around, snuggle into him when you're watching a movie. Allow him to place his arm on the church pew or sofa behind you, but be careful. If you rest your head on his shoulder, your lips are close and inviting—and this could tempt a kiss.

If Hold Close and Kiss is your boundary, be careful! This one is challenging because there's only one boundary left before Have Sex. Instead of kissing on the mouth, drop a kiss on his forehead or blow him a kiss as you leave the room. Rub your noses together in an Eskimo-kiss. Kisses on the cheek are sweet. Let him kiss your hand if he's so inclined. Chivalry is not dead.

Temptation abounds when we cross into Further Physical Contact. It's dangerous emotionally as well as physically, since some STDs are passed through genital contact. My goal is to keep you safe in all aspects—emotionally, physically and spiritually. I don't recommend setting your boundary at Further Physical Contact.

............................................................

A worthy man respects the boundary.

............................................................

Justin proved that a worthy man respects the boundary.

He preserved more than my virginity that night I tempted him. He guarded my heart and protected my soul. Engaged or not, we weren't married. Dating for two years didn't matter. I'm so thankful for his decision to uphold our boundary.

Our wedding was amazing, but our wedding night was incredible. We share a beautiful memory, and I absolutely believe, without a shadow of a doubt, that God blessed that night because we waited.

So, if you're not having sex and making out, what is there to do? Let's see, the best part of being in a relationship is the "being together" part. And being together is sometimes enough for anything.

I proved this when I would wake up early to meet Justin for a run.

I hate running. I hate waking up early. But when we were dating, I'd wake up at 5:30 every morning just because I couldn't get enough of him. Knowing that he was waiting for me gave me more energy than Starbucks' double shot espresso madness.

Remember my friends David and Mallory? They understood this concept of togetherness. David said of dating Mallory, "I loved how we could have fun doing anything. Whether it was a nice dinner-and-movie date or just a night of take-out and a cheesy movie rental, we always made it fun together."

## Tangible Reminder

Ah, my darlings. Here we come to the crux of the matter. We're overloaded with warnings of the physical consequences: pregnancy, STDs, sterilization as a result of certain STDs; but we need to dive into the emotional ramifications if we don't stick to a boundary that's pleasing to God.

Shame. Ridicule. Judgment. Hurt. Jealousy. Feeling used and taken advantage of. Rejection.

*Jesus, take the wheel.*[2]

Not only have I felt the indignity of lowering my standards and riding waves of regret, I've counseled numerous other girls after they bobbed their heads in the apple bucket of "going too far" and came up sputtering and feeling empty and foolish. It hurts to know that a guy has experienced part of your heart, wadded up the memory and tossed it in the trash. It's worse when he throws it to the ground, calls his buddies around to watch and stomps on it, digging his heel into the dirt as he twists, turns and does a little jig.

Holding hands can cause enough thrills to last quite a while, and once he puts his arm around you, it's heaven. Kissing is amazing and, frankly, should be *as far* as it goes until your wedding night. Jase Robertson from A&E's hit show *Duck Dynasty* says, "Kissing and touching above the neck only. Everything else waits until you're married." He is absolutely right. *If you're not watching this show, I promise you will love it.*

How realistic is this? Come on, it's the twenty-first century. Sex is no longer a taboo topic; it's a pastime for many teenagers. The bridge from kissing to sex is slippery, shifty and scary. As soon as you start down the path, you can go from zero to *what-was-I-thinking* in no time flat. There is no going back, and like my husband says, there are some things you can't come back from . . . some things you can't undo.

Bruised hearts hurt worse than slapped faces, so guys usually get the better end of a broken romance. It's one thing to deal with your own sense of guilt and remorse. It's quite another to have shame waved in your face like you don't matter.

We do matter.

You matter.

Giving a guy access to your physical charms is a dangerous hunting ground. It's like giving a hungry wolf a taste of blood, hoping he won't spring for the kill. Our hearts are too fragile for his hands, our emotions too precious to be gifted in exchange for the warmth of his body.

· · · · · · · · · · · · · · · · · · · · · · · · · · · · · · · · · · · · · · · · · · · · · · · · ·

The cold metal of a purity ring resting on your guy's warm flesh reminds you of your promise to wait for the man who steals your breath away, not your virtue.

· · · · · · · · · · · · · · · · · · · · · · · · · · · · · · · · · · · · · · · · · · · · · · · · ·

When temptation is strong, you're close to casting aside the reality of how special God made you. He never intended for more than one man to know you, understand you, recognize you.[3] Seeing the cold metal of a purity ring resting on your guy's warm flesh reminds you of your promise to wait for the man who steals your breath away, not your virtue.

My tangible promise sits tucked away in a silver jewelry box in my husband's secret hiding spot. I gave him my promise ring—a little rough around the edges where I'd let impropriety nick the rims of innocence—an hour before we said our wedding vows. It was mine no longer. The ring I'd worn faithfully for eight years was his forever, because I was his forever. Fully, completely, absolutely.

Jesus polishes the scratches of our purity rings, fixing the dents and replating the areas rubbed off during moments of sinful exuberance. He is the Master Jeweler, and despite how far we've tiptoed, snuck or leapt over the boundaries, He lets us stand before Him as our soon-to-be husband slips a brand-new ring on our finger.

**Notes**

1. Taylor Swift, "Fifteen" (Nashville, TN: Sony/ATV Songs, DBA Tree Publishing Co. Taylor Swift Music). http://www.directlyrics.com/taylor-swift-fifteen-lyrics.html
2. Carrie Underwood, "Jesus, Take the Wheel" (Nashville, TN: Arista, 2005).
3. This keeps in mind the understanding of biblical exceptions of remarriage.

# 10

## *Kissing*

*A kiss, when all is said, what is it? . . .*
*Tis a secret told to the mouth instead of to the ear.*

EDMOND ROSTAND

I've kissed six guys in my life. The first was inevitable, the second was sweet, the third was lustful. The fourth I didn't deserve and the fifth I regret. The sixth kisser married me.

Kisser #6 is my favorite.

Three weeks after we met, Justin kissed me at his parents' house. Two years later, he kissed me at the altar. Thirty minutes ago, he kissed me goodnight.

Girls, part of me wishes that Kisser #6 had been Kisser #1 and the numbers ended there. Part of me wishes that Kisser #5 wasn't so intimate with me and that Kisser #3 never happened. I wish Kiss #4 had saved his first kiss for his wife, and I wish that Kiss #1 hadn't occurred during a putt-putt game.

My first kiss happened because of peer pressure from the guy's buddy. Once I realized what he was doing, I actually turned my head away. However, his mouth touched the edge of my lip, ever so slightly. Technically, it counted.

Yup. The long-awaited, romantic first kiss happened at the Congo River mini golf course. Hole number 8.

Kisser #2 (the kiss that was sweet) occurred after a fantastic date at Disney. We had a great day, and after exploring the Magic Kingdom, we shared a casual dinner before he drove me home.

When he pulled up in front of my house, I thanked him for a wonderful day with a quick pop-kiss goodbye. I'm not sure it actually signified a kiss, but since our lips touched for half a second, I guess it counts.

Kisser #3 (the lustful kiss) was a mistake. And it was more than a kiss—it was a make-out session in his college dorm room. On his bed. I didn't recognize myself as I took my walk of shame an hour later. I wasn't a kissing slut. Who had I become?

## Kissing Remorse

I truly regret kissing #4.

Kisser #4 was the college roommate of Kisser #1. *Yes, I know this is starting to sound like a soap opera, but hey, it's what happened.*

Kisser #4 was, and is, one of the best guys I know. He is down-to-earth, sweet and super smart. I don't know if we technically dated since it lasted such a short time, but we first held hands in the movie *Gladiator* and definitely kissed a few times.

I found out later that I was his first kiss.

And I felt horrible.

He is absolutely a great guy, but I didn't see us getting married. To be honest, I was so insecure that I was only looking out for my best interests. Through the grace of God, we remained friends. As stupid as I was back then, I wish I hadn't kissed him. While I feel special to have been part of his life, he deserves to look back at his first kiss and *not* have it be with me.

I was such an emotional train wreck my first year of college that I look back at my former self and wish I could shake her shoulders, slap her cheek and tell her to stop being so self-involved and get her act together. However, I ran from Kiss #1 to Kiss #4, never stopping to figure out who I was as I searched for value in other people.

He dated at least one other girl that I know of before meeting his wife, who is one of the sweetest, most genuine people I have the pleasure of knowing. They are absolutely perfect for each other and are raising two beautifully adorable little girls.

But I stole something precious from her. I'm in his kissing memory, and I have no business being there. I didn't deserve Kiss #4 because I wasn't worthy of being *his* Kiss #1.

........................................................................

*I wonder how many girls wish their first kiss was with their husband?*

........................................................................

When we act selfishly, our behavior creates a domino effect that robs other people of blessings. In this case, I wonder if I hadn't stepped in, if his first kiss would have been with his wife. How memorable and special that would have been. I wonder how many girls wish their first kiss was with their husband?

My best friend in high school saved her first kiss for her wedding day. Let me tell you, everyone in the room waited with baited breath as her groom bent down and their lips met for the first time. Those of us watching felt joy overflowing as we witnessed this beautiful treasure, and we erupted in applause. Do you think my friend regrets waiting? I know she doesn't.

Most of the time, girls think they are going to marry the person they are dating. We're so emotional and longing for attention and acceptance that we hold tight to our dating relationships, even if they aren't healthy. Even if we know there is something better.

## Kissing Regret

Kisser #5 played me, and I fell for it.

It happened because I needed to feel desired, and he said all the right things. His sweet nothings were salve to my broken heart. I'd recently broken it off with Justin for the second time in two years, and my world had spiraled in on me. Kisser #5 saw his opportunity, and I rebounded into his arms.

He asked me to go with him to get something to eat. I wasn't hungry, but I didn't want to be alone. We pulled in, and were sitting in the car (*don't sit in the car*) when he leaned over. I let him kiss me and immediately regretted it.

Sloppy, wet, uncaring, unemotional . . . *bleh*!

I wanted to go home.

I hated that kiss. It left me feeling robbed.

I thought he liked me. He said all the right things, and I was smitten. My kisses were precious, but he didn't care. In fact, I found out a few days later that he was seeing another girl.

I. Was. Humiliated.

Even though it was *one kiss*, I hate the way that memory makes me feel.

## Kissing Reward

We shouldn't treat kissing so casually.

A kiss is powerful. Emotional. Personal. God breathed into dust and created a man; and what is kissing besides the intimate exchange of breaths?

Kisser #6 makes my knees weak and my head spin. Kissing him is breathtaking.

Joy floods my heart and butterflies flutter in my stomach as I reminisce about my Kiss #6. He is my pursuer and his kisses are sweet intensity. Kissing him is like experiencing a secret place. Never have I felt so cherished, loved, desired and respected all at the same time.

We dated for two-and-a-half years before getting married. That's a lot of kisses! During our boundary conversation, we agreed to kiss and that would be it. After a few months, he told me that kissing strongly tempted him to go further. He hadn't set boundaries in his past relationships, and he was wise enough to realize that we had to be careful; so making-out happened rarely.

And I loved him more for that.

Even though we're married, kissing Justin is still as incredible as it was when we were dating. I get tingles when he cups my face in his strong hands and bends his head to kiss me. Marriage gives passion freedom. His kisses are just as sweet but are no longer held back. Kissing him is amazing and a perk of marriage that means kissing goes to a whole new level.

·············································································

## The Three S's of Kissing
Soft
Sweet
Short

·············································································

## Kissing 101

Kissing done right gets blood pumping and hormones racing. So if you aren't planning on having sex, why are you starting the engine? This is not fair to the guy. We girls can cool off in microseconds, but it takes longer for guys to come down from that endorphin high.

Emotionally, a kiss binds us to the guy, and we can live off that emotion for days. We replay every second in our minds, remembering the texture of his lips, the sweetness of his breath, the pressure of his mouth on ours. *Sigh*.

For a guy, it's not always the same. During that kiss, his mind is on where the kiss is leading. A friend of mine confided that for him, kissing was a "means to an end." He meant that he'd kiss a girl if she wanted, but his end goal was to sleep with her. Kissing was his means of getting into her pants. And this guy is not a dirtbag—he's fantastic. And surprise, he grew up in the church, although his late teen years weren't his best example of Christian living. What I'm getting at, ladies, is that if *he* has these thoughts, imagine what guys of lesser character are thinking.

I'm thankful for his honesty, because it gives us insight into the way guys' brains are wired. God, in His infinite wisdom, created sex as a wonderful experience for a husband and wife, and kissing is the key that starts that process. Our hearts beat faster; our blood pressure rises; those feel-good hormones called endorphins flood our veins; and our souls swell with intimacy. When we kiss, especially for a prolonged amount of time, our bodies physically react to what our hearts experience.

The difference is that girls quickly transfer that physical energy into an emotional capacity. We can kiss all day and not desire sex. But our guy can't turn off that physical energy.

He wasn't designed to.

Which is why we must be careful.

Why is this a big deal? The Bible tells us, "Do not . . . awaken love until it so desires" (Song of Solomon 2:7). That love is meant for marriage, and it's in our best interests not to tempt our guy beyond what he can bear.

········································································

Exerting self-control when it comes to kissing
shows respect to your man.

········································································

Exerting self-control when it comes to kissing shows respect to your man. Yes, he absolutely wants to kiss you, but you're still being pursued here. Until you're kissing at the altar, you must show restraint with the passion of your kisses. Even at the altar, keep it classy. Save the good stuff for later that night.

Have you ever considered that every guy you kiss might be someone else's future husband? Some of us might marry our first kiss (like my friend), but in my case, it didn't happen until #6.

## Let *Him* Kiss *You*

Remember, you are allowing your guy the opportunity to pursue you, and that includes letting him make the first move. Trust me, if he likes you, he wants to kiss you. Desire is not the issue; but sometimes guys need to work up the courage. When you kiss him, not only do you rob the guy of the opportunity to be the initiator, but you also lose the magic of *being kissed*.

Think about this: When do the bride and groom become husband and wife? Technically, when the marriage certificate is signed. However, my sister and I insist that you are married when the groom hears and acts on these words: "You may now kiss the bride."

Not, "You may now kiss the groom"!

If you've been to a wedding, you know that everyone is excited about that kiss. If the bride has a veil covering her face, the groom gently lifts it over her head and, smiling, bends his head to hers.

And the audience applauds.

We're all waiting for the kiss . . . and the reception. But really, it's the kiss (and before that, it's the look on the groom's face when his bride steps into view).

Let me be blunt here: Kissing starts the sexual process. When the groom kisses his bride, I promise you he doesn't care about the reception, the cake or the garter toss. That man is ready for his honeymoon. And what a glorious thing it is to celebrate your union as husband and wife.

When I met Justin, it had been about two years since I'd kissed anyone. I played with the idea of not kissing anyone again until I kissed my husband at the altar, but Justin's playful teasing of Eskimo kisses proved too much. In an effort to respect my wishes and push my limits, he'd softly rub his nose on mine, his eyes daring me to tilt my head even one degree toward his perfectly defined lips.

Sometimes he'd stand behind my chair, hands on my shoulders and bend his head upside down so we were eye-to-eye, nose-to-forehead. "Do you know how to tell if you're perfect for someone?" he'd ask. "If your noses fit perfectly." Then he'd smile and give me a kiss on the forehead.

We'd been dating for about three weeks when he brought me, and a couple of friends, down south to meet his parents. One afternoon, during a pool game, he bent toward me and Eskimo-kissed me. I'd had it. I was tired of not kissing him to prove a moot point to myself. For the shock value, I popped up on my tiptoes and planted a quick kiss on his mouth.

His eyes opened wide and I stepped back, hand covering my mouth. My best friend, Bonnie, who witnessed the whole thing, dropped her book on the floor. In silly schoolgirl style, I grabbed her hand, she grabbed her book, and I dragged her to the room we were sharing, leaving Justin smiling like the Cheshire Cat from *Alice's Adventures in Wonderland*.

"What are you doing?" she said.

"I don't know," I said. And we stared at each other in excited disbelief.

She stayed in the room to finish her book and I walked back out into the main room. I'd heard the phone ring and Justin's deep voice as he answered it. I saw him standing in the doorway to his parents' room, one hand holding the phone to his ear, the other arm outstretched, resting his palm on the top of the doorframe as he mindlessly rocked back and forth.

He smiled when he saw me, and I felt like a mouse caught by the cat. A cute mouse, but a mouse nonetheless. The house was eerily quiet except for the voice coming from the other end of the phone. Justin motioned for me to follow him, and we sat on the edge of his parents' bed. Justin continued to talk to his friend, but kept his eyes glued to my face. I didn't move a muscle.

With his friend still chatting away, Justin leaned toward me, questioning me, beckoning me. I smiled my permission. He bent his head toward mine and kissed me like a woman should be kissed. I'm swooning as I remember it. Letting him kiss me was incredible, and making him wait a few weeks to do it was worth it. A kiss done right makes your knees go weak—it's a good thing I was sitting down.

## Guard Your Heart

Because I had put such borders around kissing, it made every kiss special. Because Justin had to wait to kiss me, he valued each one with tender intimacy and restrained passion. My kisses weren't taken for granted, and I don't want yours to be considered anything less than exclusive delicacies.

We must be careful not to turn hugging and kissing into full-blown make-out sessions. Be careful of French kissing, and make sure your kisses (and his) stay above the neck!

••••••••••••••••••••••••••••••••••••••••••••••••••••••••••••

Hickeys: the original Tramp Stamp.

••••••••••••••••••••••••••••••••••••••••••••••••••••••••••••

Ah, necking! This was a common phrase in the early to mid 1990s. It really just means lots of "kissing and caressing."[1] Hickeys are disgusting, however. To have someone suck so hard on your neck or (fill-in-the-blank with a body part) is just gross. It takes a lot of hard suction (like a vacuum) to create a hickey—which is just a bunch of broken blood vessels bruising on the surface.

Gross.

With sex becoming the industry standard in dating, kissing has become less of a beautiful thing and more of a commonplace no-brainer. Instead of pondering the dilemma of kissing on a first date, it's become "Should I have sex on the first date"? (The answer, of course, is no.) But what about kissing?

Should you kiss on the first date?

Most people would say yes, but I think it depends on how long you've known the person. Did you meet online? Don't lock lips. Been "talking" for a while? Friends forever? If he leans in for the kiss, and you like him back, let him!

Just be careful. The wisest man to ever live, King Solomon, said, "Guard your heart for it is the wellspring of life" (Prov. 4:23). I'm going to suggest you do the same with your kisses.

Some kisses begin sweet but turn bitter in your mouth.

Dear one, choose carefully who you kiss. Let him be worthy, but make sure you are worthy too.

And when you find your Kiss #6 (or if you're fortunate, only the guy who was Kiss #1), let every kiss count.

**Note**

1. "Kissing and caressing," phrase used on Wikipedia.

# 11

## Kissing Plus

*You will be sinning against the LORD; and*
*you may be sure that your sin will find you out.*

NUMBERS 32:23

Sometimes we don't regret our sin. We regret getting caught.

I made sure I never got caught, so I thought I'd never have to tell.

I graduated high school and left college with no one the wiser.

*Your sin will find you out.*

Nope, Justin forgave me. It's forgotten.

*Be sure, your sin will find you out.*

If I tell, my sister won't trust me. My parents will be disappointed. My students won't respect me.

*And you may be sure your sin will find you out.*

It wasn't until I created the proposal chapters for this book that the excitement momentarily turned to dread. God's plan for me included writing a book, convicting me to share my dirty little secrets.

I excused myself from the family room to shower and dress for a meeting. While showering, I thought about the black words of confession on the stark white computer screen. Images flashed through my mind: Derek and me in his bedroom; Justin and me in moments of weakness; Derek and me in his dorm room; Derek and his wife's wedding picture; kissing "Kiss #4" in my dorm room. And the tears flowed. For the first time, I felt my heart break as I saw myself the way God sees sin. The pain that pierced my heart left me half bent over, the steamy water streaming down my face.

## Further Physical Contact

The boundary line separating a person from Further Physical Contact was a boundary line in the RESPECT abstinence program that Derek and I facilitated in high school. Further Physical Contact covers the area between kissing (on the mouth) and having sex. In my years of working with teenagers, I've observed that a lot of kids don't want to have sex before marriage. A lot of kids do. And a lot of kids will straddle the line, pun intended.

God didn't create us with a hard and fast brake when we are tempted to go too far. Once we get "going," our bodies want to go!

For girls, the need for sexual release isn't as extreme as it is for guys. During a make-out session, he's thinking about how to get under your clothes, probably how to take them off. His hand slides up your shirt, and maybe your hand finds its way to his belt buckle.

Every time a guy is in this situation, he's expecting completion. It doesn't matter that he knows sexual intercourse is off the table—he's hoping this will be the time you don't stop.

What about that situation seems fair, right or acceptable? Yet, some guys will use "fairness" as an excuse to bully a girl into going all the way. He'll say it's her fault he's all worked up, and she owes him. I have even heard that some guys expect their dates to "repay" them for expensive dinners.

A girl never owes sex to any guy.

Don't fall for it. A girl never owes sex to any guy.

Maaaaybe on your wedding night. But other than that, no. And just be clear, you don't really "owe" your husband sex on your wedding night. But I totally recommend it.

Emotionally, this is a hard place for girls. Once we delve into the Land of Inappropriate Touching, it's hard to stop. Falling back out of that type of behavior may make us seem like prudes. Or we have to explain why we felt uncomfortable, and that could be an embarrassing conversation.

## Reputation

It's extremely disheartening when a guy feels the urge to talk about his "conquest" with other guys. Not all guys "kiss and tell," but a lot of guys "kiss and exaggerate". A guy may not speak ill of his girlfriend, but if they break up, he may not feel the need to keep silent anymore. Word spreads quickly about how far a girl is willing to go, and that reputation is hard to shake.

A friend of mine in high school, a sweet girl, only had sex one time. But according to the rumors, she'd slept with the quarterback, the offensive line and performed other favors for the rest of the team. All false. But it was all over school that she was easy and slept around.

Unfortunately, she was reminded about that awkward night every time she heard her name whispered in the hallway. A one-time mistake resulted in a reputation of being a slut. She hadn't had sex with anyone else, but it didn't matter. She'd been branded.

A good reputation is an extremely delicate thing. So fragile. Handle with care. We are to avoid every appearance of evil (see 1 Thess. 5:22). A bad or questionable reputation can be hard to overcome. It's so important to live above reproach (see Phil. 2:15).

## The License

My youth minister Mark and his wife Stacey were my ideal couple. I wanted to be Stacey and marry a guy like Mark. I loved that he'd grab her for a kiss in the church hallway and how she loved it but was slightly embarrassed at the same time. When a predictable "Oooooh" or "PDA! PDA!" (Public Display of Affection) cry arose from the teens, he'd hold up his left hand, point to his wedding band and say "License." Then he'd bend down and give her another quick kiss.

I dreamed of a guy loving me like that.

It was nice to see that married people loved each other passionately.

Married people do whatever they want, whenever they want. Going out in public is like a field trip, and when they get home, they can hug on and touch all over, knowing that if and when passion ignites, the bedroom is close by. People who have to be "all up on" in public don't have the luxury of sexual freedom, or at least they give the impression that they don't.

When people touch a little too much or hold each other a little too tight, or when their faces are a little too close, there's an awkward tension that shoots through my back, up my neck and down my spine. It makes me wonder what they're doing in private, and then I'm embarrassed for caring in the first place.

It's uncomfortable.

When couples hang all over each other, it makes me wonder, *If they are so comfortable touching like that in public, what is their comfort level when no one is around?*

## No License, No Log Rolling

The most embarrassing make-out session was while Derek and I were watching the movie *Entrapment* at his parents' house after school. Alone.

In my mind, I was as beautiful as Catherine Zeta-Jones, with my long dark hair. We'd watched the majority of the movie behaving ourselves, but before long, we were kissing again, and then we log rolled across the living room floor like roly-polies. And that was it. Just kissing while log rolling. It looks so romantic in the movies, but in reality, it's just stupid.

The afternoon sunlight was streaming in the open curtains and creating hot spots on the carpet. I remember feeling like I had an out-of-body experience. As I looked down on myself, I thought, *What are you doing? Get up, you moron. You don't look as cute as you think you do.*

Which, to be honest, was my motivation. I wanted to feel attractive. To feel wanted. To feel beautiful.

Isn't that why most girls tiptoe down the path of promiscuity? The feelings are more than physical. In fact, the driving force for me had little to do with "how good it felt," because the guilt began to overshadow any "feel-goodness." It was the fact that Derek wanted *me*. That if I *wanted* to, I could have sex. I definitely didn't want to, but the opportunity was there if I ever felt so inclined.

Looking back, I see myself in the darkest, most evil time of my life. To continue to sin grieves the Holy Spirit, and I did not feel connected to God like I should have.

I've already mentioned the purity ring I gave to Justin an hour before we said our marriage vows. My parents gave me that purity ring on my thirteenth birthday. It's a delicate gold ring with a genuine peridot stone in the setting. It is beautiful. I wore it on my ring finger to represent my promise that I would remain a virgin until I was married. It was a promise I kept; but when Derek bought me a promise ring for our anniversary, I moved the purity ring to my right hand. It was a visual reminder that I was choosing sin.

## No License, No Log Rolling, No Leg Wrapping

On a youth trip a few years ago, Justin and another youth minister combined groups for a pizza/pool party. There were a couple of college boys there, acting as "sponsors." A couple of girls swooned the moment they saw them. Well, we wish they *had* swooned so we could have sent them to their rooms. Instead, they thought it would be fun to let the guys grab them and pull them into the pool. Lots of hands. Lots of wet skin. Lots of no layers of clothing.

We dealt with the situation and thought that was the end of it until we took both groups to get ice cream before heading back to our hotel. The girls were "missing," along with the older boys. We walked around the side of the building and saw one of our sophomore girls enfolded in the college guy's arms, with her leg wrapped around his back. My blood caught fire and Justin's ears were blowing steam. It was neither a pleasant ride home, nor an easy couple of weeks, since we decided they needed weekly "conferences" with us.

We adopted the phrase "no license, no leg wrap" as a reminder to keep hands and legs to themselves until there was a wedding ring on their fingers.

**The No-No's**
Laying on each other
Resting your head in each other's lap
Hanging out in bedrooms
Laying down together on couches or floors
Kissing in the car

## My Secret: Hypocrite Walking

I was a good kid. I was trustworthy, smart and responsible. Freedom was a perk. It was also the problem.

I was allowed to study with my boyfriend. Alone.

That's when the inappropriateness began and continued for the rest of the two years we dated. He understood that we weren't going to have sex, but that left a lot of gray wiggle room as far as "getting found out" was concerned. There weren't any consequences for groping, touching or heavy make-out sessions. Since we were both virgins, pawing at each other like playful puppies, we weren't afraid of any sexually transmitted diseases.

We spent a lot of time at his house since his parents didn't care if we were in his bedroom or not. The freedom I was thankful for then is the freedom I curse now.

Hormone surges easily overpower the guilt in your heart.

"Whoever conceals their sins does not prosper" (Prov. 28:13).

Once you cross a boundary, the gate never fully shuts behind you. You can venture out of the pasture, but the deadlock never fully bolts again when you return. Sex binds like superglue, and every sexual act tightens the pull between two souls, even if it's "just touching."

I didn't expect our foolish behavior to become routine, but we had a new hobby. Every time we were alone, we made out. Even if I would think to myself, *We're not going to do this anymore,* we did. Afterwards, I'd bang my head against the proverbial wall and my heart would scream, *Why?* I had no answer. Hormones? Maybe.

But it's more likely it was because this behavior makes young people feel like adults. In all honesty, I think we were bored.

We'd look passionately into each other's eyes, say all the right things and pretend we were in love. His parents were pretty cool with us being alone at their house, at any time; they just didn't think tenth graders were ready to be having sex.

*Ewww.*

Sex wasn't on the table.

But groping was.

Not sex.

Just making out; it's harmless.

It's not!

Every time after we had made out, I'd pray and ask God for forgiveness; but the next day, we'd be making out again. We were definitely *more* of a couple now that we'd progressed our relationship to the next level. When we were seniors, I realized that people probably thought we *were* having sex, since we'd been together so long. I'd pushed my boundary line to the beginnings of further physical contact.

I was living a lie.

In essence, I was the biggest hypocrite since the Pharisees. I say that because Derek and I both facilitated abstinence education classes, but after we left, we'd go make out in his bedroom. I firmly believe in abstinence, and I justified myself since we weren't *having sex*. Nobody questioned us, and we kept our silence.

The longer this went on, the more tumultuous our relationship grew. The problem with making out is that you no longer have to work on your relationship. We still fought, but we could "do stuff" to fix it. We were glued together by our secret and by our unwillingness to be single. We were classically codependent.

When we were 16, our youth minister, Mark, took a job in Orlando. It was one of the hardest transitions of my young life. I stayed at our local church for almost a year and put up with the new guy, George. Even if George had tried to be a good youth minister, there was little room for anyone else in my heart. Mark was like a father to me, and his wife, Stacey, was my mentor and confidante. I loved them more than anything. I found identity in youth group; and when Mark and his family left, a big part of me went with them.

Late in our senior year, George took our youth group on a youth trip and left us without supervision to go to a baseball game. When parents found out that we were un-chaperoned, he was called into a disciplinary committee meeting. George's horrid wife, in an inappropriate and desperate attempt to throw attention off of George, told the room full of parents and church elders that I was having sex.

I wasn't. Log rolling? Yes. Sex? No.

My mom, one of the parents on the committee, stood up for me and accused them of lying. It was a big "to-do," and I let her fight my fight.

I wasn't having sex, but I knew where the glimmer of truth was coming from. I was irritated with Derek for getting close to George; but after we broke up (I should say, one of the *many* times we broke up), he didn't have anyone else to turn to. I was one of Mark's, the former youth minister's, favorites, and Derek had become George's.

Shortly after George's wife's accusation, I started driving 45 minutes to the church where Mark and Stacey were now serving. I'd get up super early on Sunday mornings and drove out there most Wednesdays. Eventually, George moved his family back north. When Derek and I were "on again," he and I would ride over together.

The emotional consequences of our sexual immorality were weighing me down. I felt guilty around Mark. I felt guilty when I taught purity lessons. I felt guilty because I didn't know how to stop returning to the vomit (see Prov. 26:11).

## Repentance

I hated myself for the sin cycle I was caught in: fool around; repent; fool around; repent. It never completely stopped. There would be longer time frames in between, but I knew that God had to be tired of the same empty promises coming forth from my lips. Did He even believe me? He knew I was going to do it again, and even though my heart didn't want me to do it again, I knew it would only be a little while before moments of weakness or a need to "salvage" our relationship resurrected our make-out sessions.

My feelings of guilt during this time were immense. So many times I wanted to tell my best friend, Mandy. So many times I wanted Mark to look me in the eyes and say, "I know what you're doing, and you need to stop." I half-heartedly prayed for the sweet release the tears of repentance would bring once I confessed my sin.

Though I cried out to the Lord in my heart with sorrow and regret, I never uttered those same words of confession to anyone else. If I had confessed my sins to Mandy or Mark and Stacey, they would have prayed with me and for me so that I would be healed (see Jas. 5:16).

* * *

> Looking back, I was a girl trying to prove I was a woman to a boy trying to be a man.

* * *

Fooling around with Derek was one of the dumbest things EVER. What was the reward? Did the experience make me more valuable to another man? Quite the opposite, actually. Sexual experience cheapens you. Looking back, I was a girl trying to prove I was a woman to a boy trying to be a man.

What was the cost of my wallowing in this muck between sweet kisses and forbidden sex?

A distanced relationship with God.

The burden of carrying a secret.

Feeling like a hypocrite.

Was it worth the guilt and shame I felt when I told Justin that I'd let another man touch me and understand me in a way that was supposed to be for him only?

It's *never* worth it.

Justin demonstrated grace. After he told me about his past, I didn't feel as bad about my own, but that didn't change the embarrassment of confessing the words out loud. Instead of seeing my sin through God's eyes, he saw it through the eyes of a fellow sinner. However, God sees my sin through perfect eyes. How grateful I am that Jesus paid my debt, although my sin is trite compared to the suffering He endured.

Although my sin found me out, I stand strong behind the blood of Jesus and pure white in front of God the Father (see 2 Cor. 5:17-21). For that, I am eternally indebted.

# 1 2

# *Sex*

*How can [men] possibly use sex to get what we want? Sex is what we want.*

FRASIER CRANE

We had to have sex before midnight.

A few hours earlier, Justin helped me out of my wedding gown so we could change into less formal attire for a private dinner with my mom's side of the family.

As he undid the long zipper, he placed a soft kiss on the back of my neck.

It was strangely wonderful undressing in front of him. I felt no shame as his eyes took in my corset and layers of lacy crinoline. I slipped out of the hoop skirt as he urged me to quickly dress for dinner so we wouldn't get teased for being late.

Dinner couldn't end soon enough.

The precious time we spent with my family made up for the awkwardness I felt, knowing that every person at our table knew we were headed back to our hotel for our first night together.

My next dressing change was into a sheer ivory slip-gown with a delicate pearl-and-bead rose bloom on the hip, a present from my mom at my bridal shower. My beautiful gown of beads and lace lay carefully draped over the back of the plush sitting chair in the honeymoon suite. The tulle veil and tiara rested on a side table.

I stared at myself in the bathroom mirror before taking a deep breath. The sound of the bubbling Jacuzzi and the pop of the champagne bottle meant that Justin was ready. I gave myself a once-over and exited into the candlelit bedroom where my new husband sat waiting on the edge of the bed.

## The Birds and the Bees

There is so much I didn't know about sex.

I'd had "the talk" with my mom when I was in fourth grade. I remember thinking that if a mommy and daddy kissed a certain way, and prayed while touching the belly button, they would have a baby. I didn't know if there was a secret code that adults told each other, because otherwise people would be having babies all over the place. I thought the praying part was the key there—and touching the belly button. The belly button had to be involved.

When my mom told me what *really* happens, I gagged and fell prostrate onto the floor. Guh-ross. Sex was like plugging a cord into an electrical socket? *That's not what she said, but that's the first image that popped in my head.* How could that be fun? I knew guys were different than girls, but I had NO clue that sex involved the down-stairs region.

When I learned that sex can be messy, I thought I'd had a heart attack.

It's not the same as what they show on TV. In sitcoms, people have perfectly made beds with six fluffy pillows, and they read or do work before turning in. The husband tries to grope his wife, and she says no. Witty comment. Audience laughter. Roll credits.

Not the way it works.

So much of what I thought love and marriage was about came from what I'd seen on TV. And since most shows are the same, depicting stereotypical relationships, it's been a difficult road personally as I've learned how marriage really works.

You don't have sex every night.

Lingerie is usually not part of the process.

Morning sex is amazing.

But we don't talk about it, because it's uncomfortable and awkward and, yes, most things are private. But here's what I know: It was worth waiting for.

Justin's past doesn't haunt me any longer.

I'd won.

I didn't have sex with him while we were dating.

And he pursued me.

We didn't sleep together.

And he chased me.

We waited, and our wedding day couldn't come fast enough.

The ring on my finger serves as a promise more than simply for better or for worse. It symbolizes that *I* was worth waiting for. That he *truly* loves me.

Because true love *waits*.

## Sex Is Amazing

Instead of being the woman who steals a man's heart, you can be the one to protect it.

Justin went to breakfast with one of his minister buddies, Mack, this week. During the course of their conversation about teenage relationships, Mack told Justin about a girl he dated in high school.

"I wanted to sleep with her, and she told me no. She said, 'Aren't you wanting to be a preacher? You're not going to look back and think of me as the person who 'ruined you.'"

He took a bite of his tater tots and looked out the window. Justin sipped his Dr. Pepper and remained quiet, waiting for him to continue. "I wish I could tell her thank you. She'll never know how much not having sex affected my life."

Is sex worth waiting for?

Absolutely.

Sex is an amazing thing—it grows and develops with the range of emotions, bringing new life into each time. The Church as a whole doesn't talk about sex enough except to bash it. We make sex seem dirty to discourage premarital sex. Or we pass out condoms and tell teens to be safe. The thing is, sex in marriage is only as "dirty" as you want it to be, and the safest place there is.

Sometimes sex is so intimate, so thrilling, so deeply beautiful, it can bring you to tears and leave you breathless.

At our annual youth retreat this summer, we heard an amazing talk from Judah Smith, lead pastor at The City Church in Seattle, Washington.[1] He walked his hipster self on stage and I knew I was either gonna love him or hate him; there wouldn't be anywhere in the middle to land. I like people like that.

In his message, "Is Jesus Enough?" he talked about his relationships. He told the boys in the audience that they could cross their arms and not listen to what he says because "old guys don't know anything about sex." But then he said, "I may not look like much, but I'm married to an amazing woman. I can have sex whenever and however I want, so don't be ragging on me, playah."[2]

I cheered.

"When people say _____ is better than sex,"
I always think, *They must not be doing it right.*

If married people started "doing sex right" and not making it seem like getting married is a prison sentence—if we started celebrating the perks of marriage—maybe we could revolutionize the way young people see sex. Just maybe, if we show that waiting is best by living out the proof of waiting—by talking about it more in a positive light—we can change the perception.

Right now the perception of sex *inside* of marriage blows.

We don't talk about how amazing it is to be with one person for the rest of your life. Instead, TV portrays bachelor parties as the "final fling" before the "ol' ball and chain." I've heard things like, "I can't imagine having sex with only one person" or "I'd get so bored sleeping next to one man for the rest of my life."

I think that's crazy.

I've been married for nine years; and just as soon as I think sex can't get any more mind-blowing, the next time is even more incredible. Sex is more than just intercourse. It's two souls entwined so deeply that nothing can unravel them. Sometimes it's so beautiful it makes you cry, wrapped in the safety of your husband's arms. Sex in marriage is a safeguard to affairs, and it's the closest thing to God's passion for the Church that we'll ever understand (see John 3:29).

That's why sex outside of marriage distorts, creates pain and brings ruin.

The thought of having an affair doesn't cross our minds, because we worked hard for each other, and God blesses that reward in our marriage.

When you go to the wedding of people who have been living together, there's a sense of "they're making this right." We know this to be true because we joke about it: "She's finally making an honest man out of me."

There isn't the same excitement as when couples get married who have waited for each other. Since I've been to both kinds of weddings, I know this to be true.

When the couple has been waiting, there is a tension, an exciting current that buzzes. The bride nervously anticipates their personal after-party, and the groom can't wait to leave the reception.

It's joyous. Just like the angels celebrate salvation, I believe they rejoice at the weddings of those who have remained pure.

My sister's friends, Ben and Amy, dated for a few years, moved in together, had four kids, but didn't get married. About two years ago, they started going to church and became Christians. It totally changed their lives.

They were so serious about doing what God wanted that they decided to get married. Even more amazing, Ben moved out of the master bedroom. They wanted a wedding instead of a courthouse appointment. So while they planned the wedding, he slept on the couch.

After being together for almost two decades, I'm sure it was difficult to remain abstinent. Really, who would have blamed them for sleeping together during their engagement? These days, it's "no big deal."

But pleasing God was important to them, and their faithfulness was rewarded in a rich and happy marriage.

## Sex Binds

I'm not worried that Justin might cheat on me.

I know that when we're apart for a couple of weeks, he's not itching for release or searching for someone new. Goodness—he waited two-and-a-half years between sexual escapades. Even if we were apart for a few months, it would seem like minutes compared to before. He worked hard to get me and he's not going to throw that away.

It's like this: While you're dating, you need to work on the emotional aspects of your relationship. Of course you want to have sex . . . maybe not right away, but the sexual tension will build.

It's supposed to!

Abstaining from sex leaves room for building a mature relationship. Emotions aren't muddied up with sexual frustrations or even sexual wonders. If you're mad at your husband, make-up sex is awesome. If you're mad at your boyfriend, you can walk away.

The beauty of marital make-up sex is that you know you aren't going to break up. If you're dating, and you get mad at each other, sex clouds your brain from analyzing the fight. They say sex is 95 percent of a bad relationship and 5 percent of a good one.[3] Now analyze your relationship. If you're having sex with your boyfriend, or anyone who isn't your husband, stop!

You have to make sure the person you're dating is someone worth marrying; once sex is introduced into the equation, you're no longer thinking as clearly as you were before.

When you're dating, sometimes you need to break up with your guy. If you're not having sex, it is easier to sever a relationship than if you've bound your hearts together physically.

Justin and I broke up twice. As painful as that was, I can't imagine how much harder it would have been if we'd been having sex.

I don't understand ever wanting another man to see me naked or touch me in areas where only my husband (or my doctor!) is allowed access. I don't worry about Justin talking about our sex life to his friends, and I'm not worried that if I do something to make him mad, he won't want to have sex again.

# The Lie

The biggest lie we tell ourselves is that we can have sex when we find the *right* person. We can have sex if we *love* the person. Once we're *ready*.

How horribly subjective! It sounds special, but in reality it's deceptive. Katrina thought she was special when Justin slept with her. So did Annie, Rebecca and Jennifer.[4] Obviously, they weren't special enough for him to commit to.

Maybe they thought he was the "right one."

Obviously, he wasn't.

Perhaps they *loved* him.

So?

But they were *ready*.

What does that even mean? God put clear boundaries on when you're *ready* for sex: It's when you are married. He never gave us permission to dabble in sex based on our feelings or what we think.

He said sex is for when you are married. End of story.

As a whole, we do a horrible job discussing abstinence. We try scare tactics with stats on STDs, the hardships of teen pregnancies and the dangers of hellfire.

What about the pain when your heart is ripped away from the person you're sexually attached to? What about the pain you cause others?

What about the future wife of the boyfriend you're sleeping with?

What about Justin's one-night stands? I picture those girls walking out the next morning, or even late that same night, not realizing they had left behind a bit of their spirit. He threw that precious piece in a corner, swept some guilt on top and let cobwebs of apathy shroud the dark space. Meaningless. Cold.

Why has the delicious union of husband and wife become a tasteless pastime for people looking for acceptance, wholeness and love?

We're desensitized to the beauty of sex within God's boundaries. Sex is everywhere we look and everywhere we wish it wasn't. It's in our schools, our churches, our children's lives. Babies are having babies. Spousal affairs abound. Teen experimentation is expected.

When I was a teen, I had always thought if I had sex before I got married, I would get pregnant. I wasn't afraid of pregnancy as a punishment, even though I didn't want to have kids before I got married. No, my fear was that my sin would be obvious.

Sex in high school is no longer taboo; there's no shame attached to promiscuity. I think we had only two or three girls pregnant during my entire four years of high school. Now, the girls in my youth group mention a newly pregnant friend every few months or so. The shock value is gone.

I want better for you.

I want you to jump into your husband's waiting arms when you wave that positive pregnancy test in the air. I want you to have him hold your hair while you suffer through morning sickness; squeeze your hand during birth contractions; and kiss you when the delivery is over.

······················································

"Jumping into a relationship based on physical needs means you'll miss out on growing that relationship into something deeper" (David and Mallory).

······················································

Our media culture has given teen moms a national television platform and removed strong parental involvement in shows like *The Secret Life of the American Teenager* and *90210*. "Morality is as individual as you are" and "No one can tell you no" are the mantras of society.

Are you hoping I would get off my soapbox?

Not yet.

TV programs and movies glorify premarital sex and downplay married sex adventures. When married people have sex on-screen, they are usually unattractive parents instead of the Mr. & Mrs. Smith routine.

Sexual impurity is a sin, and it hurts the soul; but it's also a sin against your body (see 1 Cor. 6:18). We need to cultivate control over ourselves—a self-discipline the Bible refers to as a control in holiness and honor (see 1 Thess. 4:3-5). Since God's nature does not change, we know that when He says to "let the marriage bed be undefiled" (Heb. 13:4, *ESV*), He means it.

Our society, however, continually changes, and over time it has drawn a vastly different line on what is acceptable. Just look at movie rating standards. What was once an R rating is now PG or PG-13. It's crazy how low our standards have fallen.

How did we get to a place where 16-year-old girls feel so worthless that they offer blow jobs as a way to feel desired? When did we fall so low that our elementary students are having oral sex, and our schools are filled with pregnant seventh graders? Should we be surprised? Our popular songs are full of blatant sexual orders: *"Blow my whistle baby . . . we start real slow. You just put your lips together and you come real close."*[5]

How much more disrespectful of women can we become? Why does a guy assume that a girl wants to put her mouth on him?

Teenage girls and young women perform these sexual favors thinking that they are getting around the "having sex" issue. After all, you can't get pregnant from oral sex.

Honey . . . sweetie. Any time a guy says that oral sex isn't sex, ask him why the word "sex" is in the name. I had a guy try to pull this once. He showed me a picture from his dad's *Playboy* stash and said he wanted us to copy it. No, thanks.

One of the scariest STDs, in my opinion, is HPV (Human Papillomavirus). Put your hand (or mouth) on someone's *downstairs* that is infected, then touch yourself, and voila!

Guess what? Only certain strains of HPV cause genital warts, so you can't tell if someone has HPV just by looking at them. It also causes throat cancer, so your oral pleasures aren't as safe as you think.[6] The symptoms are, typically, cold or flu-like symptoms, so rarely do people even know they're infected. Some STDs can cause sterility, which means fooling around now can hurt your chances at having children later. Other STDs that are bonus gifts attached to an oral sex present include HIV, herpes, syphilis, gonorrhea, HPV and viral hepatitis.[7]

Ladies, we need to have more respect for ourselves. No matter what you've done, ask for God's forgiveness and the strength to keep your heart and body pure from this moment on.

........................................................

"Celibacy is not just a matter of not having sex. It is a way of admiring a person for his or her humanity, maybe even for his or her beauty" (Timothy Radcliffe).

........................................................

## Be Wise and Listen

None of my girlfriends who are raising kids on their own want their kids to follow in their footsteps. Parents want the best for their children, just like God wants the best for us and I want the best for you. There's wisdom behind the advice and sometimes regret hidden in the voice. When an adult opens her heart to share her experiences, do yourself a favor and listen.

No one is trying to ruin your fun. The best years of your life are the ones you're experiencing, and you need to enjoy every moment. But these years are crucial for how you set up the rest of your life. Be careful, sweetheart, who you let into your bedchamber, because marriage must be held in honor by all. Flee from youthful passions and pursue righteousness, faith, love and peace, along with those who call on the Lord from a pure heart (see 2 Tim. 2:22).

## The Pain

God knows the realm of emotional pain attached to sex outside of His plan—pain we rarely convey when we talk about sex.

I feel the emotional consequences of Justin's sexual decisions. He gave away what wasn't his to give. Those women touched him, kissed him, *knew him* in the same manner that I was privileged to know him as his wife. They stole something from me.

After we exchanged vows and rings, God gave us authority over each other's bodies. I was his and he was mine, but what we exchanged was incomplete. While God filled the gaps through prayer and repentance, He allowed us to feel the pain of our former choices.

For a while, my heart burned with anger toward the women he'd slept with. I cursed the names of the ones he remembered and slammed my fist against the wall at the ones he couldn't.

I think about his "first time" story, and while I want to laugh at his expense, I also want to scream at her and slap him at the same time.

"Why couldn't you leave him alone?" I yell at the picture I have of her in my mind. Then the face of the man I love flashes in my mind's eye. "Why did you give yourself to her?" I scream, tears streaming down my face. "Didn't you know I was waiting?" I crumple into a heap on the floor. "I waited . . ."

My anger turns to grief for what I'll never experience; sorrow for what I'll never know; heartache that the dream of me wasn't enough to make him wait. And as tears soak my cheeks, I wait for God's faithfulness and mercy to wash over me like rain.

Sexual sin is painful. I've listened to story after story of girls who believed they were in love, proved it by sleeping with a guy and found themselves broken after the relationship ended.

One of my friends was 16 when she surrendered her virginity.

"He was older, and it wasn't his first time. It hurt and felt good at the same time. When it was over, I went to the bathroom." She stopped talking, and I wondered if he had done something to her. I pictured her in a dark room with heavy curtains where only streams of sunlight could peep through the cracks.

"And?" I prompted.

"That was it," she said, shrugging. "It was over. I never saw him again."

I felt sadness. Her first time was not exciting, romantic or worth remembering. She hated herself for letting her virginity go at such a cheap price.

Sexual immorality has a long reach; I remember that its fingers beckoned to the romantic part of my teenage heart. It whispered sweet promises of true love if I inched forward into its grasp. It assured safety, "We won't go all the way," it said, while luring me with each new thrilling touch and sensation.

Sexual immorality lies.

Instead of setting your spirit free, it binds you, tainting your relationship with the stain of promiscuity. God protects us by presenting sex as a gift for the wedding night and forever afterward. He created it to be splendid and wonderful. To experience sex before marriage is similar to sneaking a peek at the Christmas presents under the tree. It's a Russian roulette of peeling back the wrapper until you've exposed just enough to see what's inside.

If your guy hasn't committed his *life* to you by *marrying* you, you are not *his*. He is not yours. Get your hands off of each other—you don't know that you'll end up at the altar.

I have several friends who broke engagements to the person they were ready to spend happily ever after with, and I say, good for them! Hallelujah for people who muster the strength to walk away before making the second biggest commitment of their lives! (*The first biggest commitment is your choice to believe that Jesus is the Christ, the Son of the living God, and to believe that He died on a cross for your sins, was buried, and rose on the third day. He appeared to friends, family and enemies before ascending into heaven, where He sits at the right hand of God [see 1 Cor. 15:3-8].*[8] *The first biggest commitment is accepting Him as Lord and Savior of your life.*)

Those who had abstained from sex were thankful they didn't have the pain or regret from that relationship—especially after they met the man they chose to exchange vows with.

Side note: If you break off the engagement, you're obligated to give the ring back unless you called off the wedding because he cheated on you. In that case, hock that sucker and buy yourself something pretty.

## God's Blessings

God has been gracious to Justin and me, letting the ghosts of the girls in Justin's past fade into distant memories for him and letting the fact of their existence vanish from my mind. When horrible thoughts of him holding someone else creep into my thoughts, my heart cries out to God like a child cries out when he's scared. I squeeze my eyes tight and pray for God to remove the thought, letting Him take it captive (see 2 Cor. 10:5). I replace that thought with the truth that Justin's refusal to have sex with me before our wedding night proved his love for me.

Justin's blessing was that God made his heart new. The women from his past are like tiny scars, barely noticeable and hardly there. What God has joined together, let no man separate (see Mark 10:9).

Not even with lurking memories.

Regardless of your past, I believe that God will bless you when you choose to be faithful. No matter what you've experienced, you can look into your husband's eyes knowing that your wedding night will be a night to cherish. Sex is God's gift to us, and on our wedding night, we get to experience His present with no boundaries, no fear of rejection and no shame.

God's blessings are for all of us. We have no condemnation under Christ, therefore, we are a new creation (see Rom. 8:1). We don't have to drag our sexual sins around, keeping them strapped to our legs, holding on for dear life. You throw them off every time you resist the temptation to sleep with someone who isn't your husband. Every time you refrain from showing your love for your boyfriend physically, you protect his heart for him and for his future wife. You may become his Mrs. to love forever, but until that day, your love is demonstrated in your ability to wait.

I know that God's gift for Justin and me that night was the gift of forgetfulness. There were no ghosts intruding from our past; we only had each other. It was the most beautiful night in the entire world. And while it was my first drink from that cup, Justin said he'd never experienced anything like it. For this one night, God blocked his memory and let Justin love me like it was his first time.

I think God will give this gift to anyone who is willing to wait, to anyone who is willing to stop having sex until he or she is married. And even if you're already living with someone, even if you've had sex too many times to count, God will bless your obedience to become abstinent for now and surrender to His plan for marriage. It's the best wedding present you could ever receive.

**Notes**

1. See The City Church, http://thecity.org.
2. Recorded from memory.
3. I don't know who "they" refers to, but this line is quoted on Pinterest boards, discussion forums, Twitter . . . I wasn't able to find a direct source, but I love the idea!
4. These names have been changed.
5. Flo Rida, "Whistle" (New York: Atlantic Records, 2012).
6. Martin Downs, "Health & Sex: 4 Things You Didn't Know About Oral Sex," WebMD. http://www.webmd.com/sex-relationships/features/4-things-you-didnt-know-about-oral-sex (accessed September 23, 2012).
7. Ibid.
8. John 7:1-5 discusses Jesus' siblings trying to get Him to go to Judea, where the Jews were plotting to kill Him. They did not believe in Him at this time. After the resurrection, Jesus appears to his half-brother James, who becomes a believer and pens the book of James in the New Testament. http://www.jesuscentral.com/ja/james-jesus-brother-faq.html (accessed March 4, 2013.

# 13

*Exit Strategy*

*How can I be reasonable? To me our love was everything and you were my whole life. It is not very pleasant to realize that to you it was only an episode.*

W. SOMERSET MAUGHAM

When Justin and I started dating, I told him there were two reasons I would break up with him. If either of those things happened, we were history. There would be no second chances. Even as I spoke the words, I prayed that I'd never have to prove the validity of my ultimatum.

"You can never hit me, not even a playful punch," I said. "And you can never cheat on me."

"I'd never do either of those things," he told me. And he never has and never will.

Ladies, never forget that we're in the business of being pursued. Clue your guy in to your deal breakers. Men are not mind readers. While my "hitting and cheating" clause should be a no-brainer, I told Justin up front. I didn't want to be married to a man who hit or cheated, so I refused to date a guy who would do either.

## Deal Breakers

Just like we talked about making a list of your qualifications for guys, you need to have a mental list of reasons you will walk away from a relationship. You need to date with your eyes wide open. (Unless he's kissing you, of course.) Here are some questions you should be able to answer about your man:

What's his first reaction when he finds something valuable that isn't his?

What's his rating limit for movies and video games?

Is he comfortable going to strip clubs?

Would he be okay if his friends hired a stripper for his bachelor party?

How does he treat his mother/sister when he's angry?

How does he treat you when he's upset?

Dating is the trial run, honey, and if your man can't pass the test, you don't give him a red ribbon for almost winning. Toss him a white ribbon for participating, and send him on his way. You have to think with your heart and love with your head.

I can hear some of you now. *That doesn't make any sense, Bethany. You can't think with your heart, Bethany. You can't love with your brain, Bethany.*

. . . . . . . . . . . . . . . . . . . . . . . . . . . . . . . . . . . . . . . . . . . . . . . . . . . . . . . . . .

Thinking with your heart means you
don't give in to foolishness.

. . . . . . . . . . . . . . . . . . . . . . . . . . . . . . . . . . . . . . . . . . . . . . . . . . . . . . . . . .

I say "thinking with your heart and loving with your head" means you remove yourself from lines such as, "What the heart wants . . ." "We can't help who it is we fall in love with," "Let your heart be your guide," and "follow your heart." No, follow your brain. We're not animals, savages or barbarians. Of course we can choose who we love. Love is a verb. It's a choice. It's not out of our control.

Now, there is no denying the almost magnetic attraction you can feel for someone. I know, because I was instantly attracted to Justin. But that didn't mean that my heart took over and I stopped being rational. That's why it's so important to set boundaries and know your deal breakers, because in the heat of the moment, you have to squelch the feelings and listen to reason.

So set up boundaries, like we talked about in chapter 9. When those lines are crossed, the big guns come out. Thinking with your heart means you don't give in to foolishness. It means that when your back is against the wall and you're faced with a deal breaker, you have the courage to follow your good sense.

Sometimes I wish there were a magic wand that allowed us to know if we've found "the one."

Do your eyes sparkle when you talk about your boyfriend?

Do your cheeks get flushed when he walks in the room?

Does he build you up and tell you how amazing you are?

Does he encourage you to pursue your dreams?

Does he make you want to be a better person?

It's imperative that in the midst of lovey-doveyness, you maintain your "walk away" power. While you may be in a serious, committed relationship, you are still a free commodity. Sometimes it's not until the relationship is over that you can look back and realize you were *never* "in love."

Dating is messy because people are messy. But I'd rather wade through the muck before a life vow binds me to the mire. The only way a man is assured that you are his completely is when he meets you at the altar, the two of you exchange vows and he gets to kiss you for the first time as Mr. and Mrs.

Don't settle for what is good and miss out on what is great.

## Break-Up Reason: Not Right for Each Other

Derek and I were not right for each other. We knew it, but we were just too afraid to say goodbye. It takes a lot of maturity to say to someone, "I love you enough to leave." I would have been settling for Derek. He never pursued me, and the result was a relationship of convenience.

Love always seems real at the time you're involved in it. While I may have loved him, I wasn't *in love* with him. And I'm sure he wasn't in love with me, either.

We dated for over a year before he kissed another girl at summer camp and swore his love for her. My heart was broken, but I took him back. We spent the next year on-again, off-again.

Constantly fighting.

Insidiously miserable.

Since we'd been dating for so long, I didn't think anyone else would have dated me. At least, that's the lie I comforted myself with.

There were times when I knew exactly how my life would turn out if we got married. I'd be taken care of: we'd drive nice cars, live in a nice house and never really want for anything. We'd host and attend dinner parties, drink beer (not me) with friends on game days and lead quiet lives.

I dreaded it.

My life would be routine, seemingly perfect, but loveless and boring. I craved passion, excitement and adventure. I wanted to be with someone who wouldn't be embarrassed when I found humor in life's oddities. With all the issues we'd had with Derek's cheating on me, I foresaw marital affairs and a potential divorce. He wasn't the man God intended for me, and likewise, I wasn't the woman God intended for him.

Even after we broke up, I still thought about him all the time. He stayed at Florida State University, and I came home. In my mind, he was living the life I'd dreamed of, and I'm still jealous of his FSU alumni status. What if I'd bought the lie that loving someone meant not being able to get him out of your head? I may have convinced myself that God meant for us to be together when, in reality, God moved me across the state to get me away from him.

God gave me Justin, who loves my Ed Hardy Chucks, thinks it's cute when I'm clumsy and prefers me in shorts and a ponytail. He gives me adventure, excitement and passion. Not a day goes by that I'm bored or unloved. I can't get enough of him.

## Break-Up Reason: He Takes You for Granted

I touched on my first break-up with Justin in chapter 7.

A man should never take you for granted. Once he's used to your presence and doesn't think twice about your feelings, the pursuit is over. If you're dating a guy who doesn't thank you for the small things you do, expect similar treatment in your marriage.

Yes, I'm dragging out my soapbox again.

Do not, and I repeat, do not clean your boyfriend's room, house, car and so on. If his mother didn't teach him to stay tidy, you might as well walk away or get used to picking up dirty socks and wet towels every day of your married life. He should want to impress you, not think you are going to clean up after him. It's nice to be helpful, but taking on the role of wife and mother while you're still his girlfriend is an invitation for him to take you for granted.

## Break-Up Reason: He Hits

One of my deal breakers with Justin was that I would break up with him if he hit me. Included in that was play punching, although he thinks a pat on the tush is funny. I didn't want him to see me as "one of the guys," and I didn't want to ever be a victim of physical abuse. If a guy play hits you, what will he do if he gets angry? He may never intend to hurt you, but in his frustration, he might hit a little too hard. I wanted my guy to never be in the habit of punching. It is *never* okay for him to hit you. Allow it once, and it will continue.

One time, Justin accidentally hit me in the face. We were trying to get out the door and were standing really close together when I saw something on the floor. He turned around to say something to me at the exact moment I bent down to retrieve whatever it was. Pop! Right on the cheek. It hurt so bad that I started to cry, which is always unpleasant after you've done your makeup.

I remember thinking that if my face hurt this badly as the result of a legitimate accident, I couldn't imagine letting him hit me with full-force, or even half-force. He felt horrible, especially when I teasingly threatened to tell everyone that he gave me a knuckle sandwich. Thankfully there was no bruise, but Justin's heart ached that he'd hurt me. After giving me a couple of kisses, we headed out the door.

A real man caresses a woman's cheek, gently holds her hand and brushes her hair out of her eyes. He doesn't threaten to hurt her, or lift his hand against her.

If you're in a relationship with a guy who thinks it's okay to hit you, sweetheart, you need to find help. A man who hits you will never stop. It is a sequence of anger, hitting, silence and then remorse. Don't let the cycle even start. Find a trusted adult and tell him or her. Most major cities have shelters that can hide you. The national hotline number is 1-800-787-3224.

## Break-Up Reason: Lack of Character and Integrity

Abraham Lincoln said, "Character is like a tree, and reputation like a shadow. The shadow is what we think of it; the tree is the real thing."

Does your man have integrity? Does he put other people's comforts ahead of his own? Does he do the right thing, even if he gets the short end of the deal? You can tell a lot about a man (or woman) by how he treats the person who can do nothing for him. It's in our human nature to bend over backward with kindness toward someone who can get us ahead in life—a boss, teacher or celebrity. But how a person treats the waiter, the cashier, or the bag boy after his bread gets squashed by the milk speaks volumes about his true character.

I was on a movie date with a guy when he found a wallet on the sidewalk on our way to the ticket center. He opened it up to look for identification. There was no ID, no cash and nothing really of interest. He was about to put it in his pocket when I asked him if he was going to turn it in. He played it off like "Of course I'm going to turn it in," but I'm not sure he was.

I declined his second date invitation.

A man who acts shady with small things will have no problem taking a risk with serious issues.

## Break-Up Reason: He's a Cheater

Every year, our youth group played in a statewide church football tournament. One year, I arrived late to the first night's session because I had to cheer at a basketball game. When I entered the auditorium, I saw an empty seat next to Derek. How sweet that he had saved me a seat in the crowded room.

I gave him a kiss on the cheek and listened to the speaker. When the session ended, my friends asked me about the other girl. *What girl?* Apparently, Derek had spent the majority of the evening with a girl from another youth group, and she'd been sitting in the seat I thought he'd saved for me.

They pointed her out. She had dark wavy hair and was about my height and shape. I hated her. But I felt superior because I was still wearing my cheerleading uniform. *Remember my insecurity issues?* I remained close to Derek the rest of the night, catching her eye a few times and sticking my chin up at her while my friends gave her the evil eye.

The next day, Derek found several opportunities to talk to her. I was fuming. It was Valentine's Day weekend, we'd been dating for almost two years, and yet he got her phone number. He apologized by giving me the overstuffed white teddy bear and roses he'd hidden in his trunk.

Fool me once, shame on you.

Five months later, he kissed that girl at a weeklong retreat and told her he loved her. They'd been emailing each other every day since they'd first met. My heart was crushed.

Fool me twice, shame on me.

But we got back together.

If I'm completely honest, Derek was security wrapped up in hormones. What I thought at the time was that love is incomparable to what true love is.

Don't follow in my footsteps.

This girl became a source of contention for the next year. He said they weren't emailing, but I'd find emails. He said they weren't talking, but I'd find out they were. Even in college, they were still keeping in touch. "She means nothing to me," he pleaded when I threatened to break it off. "She's just a friend. I love you." And then he'd kiss me, and I'd forgive him.

I wish there was a clever saying about not learning your lesson the third time, but there isn't.

Eventually, he married her.

Once a cheater always a cheater? I'd say yes, but that would negate God's work in those who cheated once and never cheated again. With God, all things are possible, but I vowed that I would not be cheated on again. The "one time and you're out" mentality was safer.

································································

True love is indescribable.

································································

Bottom line: If a man cheats on you when you're dating, what stops him from cheating when you're married? Kick that dirtbag to the curb and save yourself boxes of tissue and puffy, red eyes.

## My Breaking Point

True love is indescribable.

People have tried to sum up the overwhelming emotions, but how do you capture the flutter of your heart when he smiles at you, the tingle down your spine when he touches you, or the calm that passes over you when you get a whiff of his cologne as he walks by? I'm not the only one who has slept with a guy's shirt, breathing in the rich aroma of him and cuddling with it night after night until all the goodness has been smelled out of it.

I've mentioned that Justin and I broke up after dating for eight months because I thought he was taking me for granted. A year later, he pushed me to the breaking point again.

His Marine Corps unit offered him an Active Duty Reserve position, which he accepted, moving him from the Christian college back to his home in south Florida. Somehow we were able to meet up once a month; either he had a weekend off to drive up to Orlando, or I'd spend the weekend at his parents' house.

About six months after he'd accepted the position, Justin received a long-weekend pass and drove up to see me. Even though I was no longer working at the school, I met him on campus since he was spending the night with his friend. I figured we could hang out in the Student Union building (SUB), play some pool, eat dinner and maybe watch a movie. After he hugged and kissed me hello, he grabbed his overnight bags out of the car and took them to his friend Jordan's room. He didn't come back out.

I knocked on the door, unable to go inside due to the strict boy-girl policy in the dorms. He came out, explained that he was going to play some video games with Jordan, gave me a perfunctory kiss on the forehead and shut the door. I stood there for a minute, processing what had just happened.

We hadn't seen each other in a month, and he'd rather *play video games*? With *Jordan*? I went to my car, grabbed the Silver Sabre (the pool stick he'd given to me at Christmas), and marched to the SUB to take out my aggression on the pool table.

A game was in progress, so I called dibs and sat down to watch, screwing the stick together and making small talk with some of my friends. They asked after Justin and I smiled bravely and explained that he was hanging out with Jordan for a little while.

You're about to meet Kisser #5.

A couple of older guys sat on the other side of the pool table, playing against my friends. I recognized Kurt from Mark's old church. We'd met at a summer conference and a combined youth outing. His friend was cute—tall and rugged. Kurt nodded his head at me, and then whispered to his cute friend who was giving me the once-, no, make that the twice-over.

Kurt came over and introduced his buddy Evan. He'd been in the Army for a couple of years and had just transferred to the college. It was a story similar to Justin's. I smiled, welcomed him to the campus, and then walked over to the pool table where it was my turn. Kurt and Evan had won their game, so my buddy Matt partnered with me for the next one. I could feel Evan's hot eyes on me as I walked. Furious at Justin for ignoring me, and gratified at Evan's obvious interest, I made sure to lean way over the pool table as I took my shots while making sure my shirt didn't open *too much* as I calculated the ball's trajectory.

I remained elusive to his questions, answering smartly and making him laugh at the appropriate times. I saw the attraction in his eyes and let him walk me out. I decided not to let Justin know I was leaving. Our relationship was a bit strained from the distance, and his avoidance set me over the edge. Evan and I stood under a street lamp, the light highlighting his blond hair. I had referenced Justin in an earlier conversation, and Evan revisited it.

"If I was your boyfriend, I'd never spend the night hanging out with a dude." The needed affirmation filled my ears. Evan's flattery dripped with sweetness, and I forgot that too much sugar can make you sick.

He asked for my number; but even though I was annoyed at Justin, I still wanted him to be the only guy I ever gave my number. So I asked Evan for his instead.

He told me to call him in 20 minutes. I agreed and walked to Bonnie's apartment. She fell asleep seconds after letting me in. When I heard her even breathing, I dialed Evan's number and hid under the covers to mask the sound of my voice from waking her.

Justin and I spent the next day together. I didn't tell him about Evan, and I felt myself being pushed further and further away from him. We argued over stupid things, and I was more confused than ever when he went back to West Palm.

Our relationship had come to a standstill.

We didn't have a next step except to get married, and we weren't ready to do that. My heart was confused. If I loved Justin so much, why was Evan on my mind? I saw Evan at the school again, and the butterflies and tingles that before I'd only felt for Justin were back.

## Be Careful of Your Counsel

It's easy to look at other people's relationships and point out the flaws and the things you would do differently. Third-party observations are usually reliable, dependent upon the source's affection for you and your main squeeze.

I didn't know what was going on with the whirlwind of thoughts and emotions, so I talked to my former youth minster Mark about it, even though he didn't like Justin (*I have never really understood why*). My friendship with Mark was a major source of contention between Justin and me. I often was torn between the man who was my mentor, surrogate father and trusted friend, and the man I loved with every fiber in my being.

It's wise to listen to the people who love you. A third-party observation is worth taking the time to hear, because they can see your relationship with a perspective you don't have.

Mark's eyes lit up when I said I might have feelings for another guy. He suggested that if I really loved Justin, I wouldn't be thinking about Evan the way I was. I was more confused than ever, but the more I listened, the more his words made sense. I knew Mark was looking out for my best interests.

While I was talking to Mark, Justin called. I hit the quiet button on my cell phone so my conversation with Mark wouldn't be interrupted. But Justin called right back, so this time I answered. With Mark's approving nods, I mustered the courage to tell Justin I didn't think I could see him anymore and, no, I couldn't attend the Marine Corps Birthday Ball that next weekend.

Sick to my stomach, but desperate for Mark's approval, I didn't answer Justin's phone calls for the rest of the night or the next day. Until now, we'd spoken every day since we had started dating, even during Justin's military training weeks. I knew Mark would be proud if I stayed strong, although my heart stung.

I thought I was going to marry Justin, but I was so confused. When he chose Jordan over me, and I felt crush-like symptoms when I saw Evan, I wondered if maybe it was time to be single again. What if I married Justin and realized years down the road that I should have married someone else? This was my last chance to see if I was compatible with another guy.

I didn't want to wake up one morning, look in the mirror and see a middle-aged woman who partied too hard trying to relive her youth. So we stayed broken up while I tried to figure everything out.

I missed Justin, but I didn't miss how he took me for granted.

Meanwhile, Evan and I talked for a couple of hours every night. He told me about his parents and family down south. He asked me about myself and always said the right things. Looking back, I can see that Evan was feeding my primary love language: words of affirmation.1 I enjoyed every word. He built me up, and I was happy. And confused. And sad.

But pretty words ease the mind, and I wrapped myself in the sweet bliss of denial. *Evan* wouldn't have stayed in another guy's room after not seeing me for a whole month. *Evan* didn't argue with me. *Evan* this. *Evan* that. I missed Justin, but I didn't miss how he took me for granted.

One night, Evan asked me to go out to eat with him. He'd changed after his basketball practice and was starving. I wasn't hungry but wanted to spend time with him. We drove separately to the KFC/Taco Bell (aka. Ken-Taco) near the school. He pulled into the parking spot next to my car and motioned for me to come sit with him. I slid into the passenger seat and shut the door. He told me I looked pretty and then said, "I really want to kiss you."

*I'm sure my eyes went wide. I hadn't kissed anyone but Justin for the last two years. We were broken up, but we were still talking. Doubts rushed into my head, but my heart urged me to take a chance and live a little. Relient K's song "Pressing On" was playing, and as I listened to the words, they were literally telling me what to do: "And I won't sit back and take this anymore, 'cause I'm done with that, I've got one foot out the door. And to go back to where I was would just be wrong. I'm pressing on.2*

I pressed on.

I nodded, and he leaned toward me. I tilted my head toward his shoulder and he pressed his mouth on mine. Instead of Justin's familiar intoxicating kiss, I felt like I'd just made out with the Saint Bernard from the movie *Beethoven*.

It lasted only a few seconds, but a few seconds longer than I wished. As soon as he pulled away, my heart dropped into my stomach. We got out of the car and went inside. I felt numb and cold, even in the Florida 80-degree humidity. He ordered his food while I sat at a table, and then I watched him eat.

Suddenly, I was comparing him to Justin, and Evan fell short. The glaze was gone from my eyes; the veil had lifted. After he inhaled his food, we went back to the college. I had to organize a few things in my car before I left, and he stood in the parking lot with me while I moved things around. His phone rang, and instead of excusing himself, he stayed within earshot.

He was talking about me to the guy on the other end of the call. He winked at me and then said, "I don't know if I've got either of them yet."

*Either of them. Yet.*

I'd heard that he had gone to a party at a high school girl's house, and stayed past the college's curfew a few nights, but I didn't know if it was true. He stupidly confirmed that rumor.

I was such a fool.

I drove home, lay down in my bed and cried myself into a fitful sleep. The next morning, I awoke with a sense of dread.

I knew without a shadow of a doubt that Justin was the man I loved forever. No other guy compared to him, no other man would ever cause my heart to be moved. The knot in my stomach grew tighter as I knew my window of opportunity to catch Justin on his commute to the base was closing.

I had to tell him what I'd done. This was not a secret to spring on him years after we were married.

He answered the phone and I started to cry. I told him I'd kissed Evan, and he was eerily silent—the calm before the storm. The edge in his voice sliced my heart with every word. He threatened to drive up and have a "talk" with Evan. He was itching for a fight, and I prayed his fellow Marines could calm him down, maybe keep him from leaving. I begged him to stay where he was, but I mistook his anger at Evan as forgiveness for me. I was dead wrong.

For the first time in our relationship, he screamed at me, "I don't want to talk to you or see you EVER AGAIN. You made your bed, now lie in it." And he hung up the phone. I stumbled into my bathroom and crumpled to the floor. I lay in a pathetic heap, tears soaking the bath rug as my sobs shook my body until I hurt from the uncontrollable heaving. It felt like a scene out of a movie, except the pain was mine.

After a few minutes, I dialed his sister's number. I told her I'd done something horrible, that Justin was on his way here and to please stop him. I was driving down immediately. I made arrangements with my job and got in my car as fast as I could.

He didn't want to see me, but he was too much of a gentleman to leave me standing by my car, crying, desperately asking for his forgiveness. We went to Applebee's for dinner, talked, and he forgave me. He told me he'd taken another girl to the Birthday Ball, a girl from his church that his mom had set him up with. He'd kissed her the next day during a picnic date, but right away realized the same thing I had when Evan kissed me.

He was still in love with me.

We were no longer each other's last "first kiss," but we'd made it through the final obstacle in our path. I learned that there are different levels of "knowing" in love.

I knew I wanted to date him.

I knew I could possibly marry him.

I knew I loved him.

I knew I was in love with him.

And now I *knew* without a shadow of a doubt that there would never be another man for me. Mark was wrong about Justin. I'd found my soul mate, and I would never take him for granted again.

While I regret the intense pain I put him through, Justin said he's glad I broke it off. When I look back, I see how close I was to losing him forever, but Justin sees this as the defining moment of our relationship, the moment when he, too, realized that he *knew*.

He couldn't risk losing me again, couldn't chance another guy stealing me away. He wanted to be my last "last kiss."

## Resolution

I don't want any misunderstanding concerning our breakup. It lasted a few horrible weeks, sending me into a tailspin of creating online dating profiles, and into a rebound kiss with Evan. It cost me never-ending days in a zombie-like state and countless nights of crying myself to sleep.

I didn't break up with Justin to manipulate him or control him. I wasn't giving him an ultimatum. I didn't expect him to propose only a few short weeks after we'd reconciled.

There comes a point in every dating relationship where you have to, for lack of a better expression, "poop or get off the pot." We'd reached this standstill and let our relationship grow stagnant.

Breakups are hard, but sometimes they are necessary. A word of caution: My plea for you is to protect your heart. Don't play around with breakups like Derek and I did. On-again, off-again isn't healthy. Don't threaten a breakup to get what you want. Only break up if you're done for real. And don't let a guy kiss you if you're not getting serious—Evan eventually married that *other* girl.

I'm thankful that God brought Justin and me back together. I'm more thankful than I can ever express.

**Notes**

1. Gary D. Chapman, *The Five Love Languages: The Secret to Love That Lasts* (Chicago, IL: Northfield Publishing, 2010).

2. Reliant K, "Pressing On" (Nashville, TN: Gotee Records, 2001).

# 14

# Engagement

*Whatever our souls are made of, his and mine are the same.*

EMILY BRONTË

Girlfriend, you made it!

You protected your heart, allowed yourself to be the prize, and some lucky man gets to spend the rest of his life with you. Aren't you thrilled? Have you torn through wedding magazines and started online dress shopping?

Engagement is such a fun time. You float on clouds as you set the foundation for the rest of your lives together. Ahhh. Just thinking of changing my last name to Justin's set my heart aflutter.

Engagement is a time when you can relax and spend your time choosing a venue, tasting cakes and registering for presents with the fun point-and-shoot registry gun. You don't have to stick to the rules any longer.

False.

Until you're married, you have "walk away" power. You are still the prize. You are still being pursued. Your fiancé doesn't get a free pass for bad behavior. Although if you've accepted his proposal of marriage, the homework's been done, and you can close your eyes for a few minutes. But not for long, there's a wedding to plan!

## Your Wedding Revolves Around You

Being engaged is glorious.

I remember that I would stick my left hand out the window when I was driving and admire the sparkle of the sun glinting on the diamonds, a surge of love shooting through my veins.

You can't help but flash your ring at everyone, paste pictures of it all over Facebook and lose the ability to talk about anything but your wedding.

Wedding planning can be exhausting, especially toward the end when you can't stand the sight of bows, tulle and wedding invites any longer. But what girl doesn't grab as many wedding magazines as she can stuff into her hands as soon as she gets the ring? *Some of my youth girls have expansive Pinterest boards dedicated to their big day. I'm totally jealous that it wasn't invented for mine!*

They say every girl dreams about her wedding from the time she is a little girl, and if that is you, I think it's fabulous. But it wasn't me. I knew I wanted to get married; but in college, I got afraid that maybe God's plan for me didn't involve marriage. And then I met Justin. *I wish I could insert the cute little Facebook heart here.* <3

Planning my wedding was wonderful. Let's be honest, the best part of being a bride is having the majority of the wedding *your way*. I knew I wanted to get married at my home church, but besides the venue and the groom, I didn't know exactly what I wanted. Which meant everyone wanted to share their ideas.

Remember, your wedding is *your* day.

Yours.

When your maid-of-honor dyes her hair cheetah orange two weeks before the wedding, take a deep breath and remember that it's your day.

When the person you've dreamed of performing your ceremony hurts your heart and you have to find someone else worthy of the honor, remember that it's your day.

When a bridesmaid backs out at the last minute and you have to awkwardly ask someone to fill in, remember it's your day.

No matter what happens, God can work through the awkward, uncomfortable, inevitable mishaps that arise when planning a wedding.

No matter how your wedding turns out, remember, you are the one who will remember everything, so don't let anyone talk you into something you're going to hate. My greatest piece of advice? Splurge on a videographer. There was so much I never got to see, people I didn't get to hug and parts of the ceremony I missed since I was the last one to enter the sanctuary. Our wedding video is one of my treasured possessions, and if I were to die young, I envision Justin sitting on our couch, video on loop, crying his eyes out as he mourns me.

> You are the one who will remember everything, so don't let anyone talk you into something you're going to hate.

*You can roll your eyes, but I'm being totally serious.*

Before I experienced engagement, I used to be horrified at the jokes about future grooms and how men just need to go along with whatever the bride wants because it's "her day." I mentally stamped my foot and thought *It's the guy's day too.* Indignant.

Until, that is, the beautiful ring was placed on my finger and the man of my dreams asked me to be his forever. After the hugs, kisses and beaming smiles from the congratulations, the planning started and I realized something.

Every decision gets bounced off the bride. Every decision must be made by her unless she's given someone else complete authority to make decisions. Even then, everyone consults the bride.

No other person will think back to your wedding as often as you will, with as much analyzing of the details, as you will do. No one will care like you will.

No one else will remember the things that went wrong and the wonderful things that went right. No one else will care in 10 years about the flower arrangements or if the service went a little out of order.

For all of my sweetheart's suggestions, I think we took, well, none of them. I did let him choose if he wanted to wear his military dress blues, but I may have persuaded him in that direction.

I'm thankful that I married a patient, giving man who, I believe, was a bit relieved to let the responsibility of planning the day of our lives fall on my shoulders. He said he got annoyed when I would ask his opinion after telling him what we were going to do. Like it was my nice way of involving him. "This is what we're doing. What do you think?" Then he mocked me, "Because we're already doing it."

In spite of my so-called selfishness, the details came together nicely. During our bridesmaid dress shopping, my friend saw these beautiful light pink strapless dresses that closely mirrored my bridal gown. They were perfect. And the centerpieces were simple and elegant. My mom worked out the food details with her friends, so everything went smoothly.

Long engagement or short, it's a fun and stressful time, and I was thankful it only lasted for six months. I don't know how I would have handled a longer engagement. So many plans to work out and the rush of the deadline spurred us to get things done.

While engagement is a time of cake tasting, dreaming and trying to lose 20 pounds, it's a relaxing time when it comes to your relationship. You've observed and dealt with the hard issues, and now you get to plan the rest of your life.

## The Dress

I scoured the magazines for the perfect dress. After all, every eye would be on me, so I had to look beautiful and perfect. I printed pictures of what I wanted and brought them with me to the first trying-on-the-dress session. To be completely candid, I wanted to close my eyes while I pulled a beautiful gown over my head and experienced that "aha" moment that brides talk about as soon as I opened my eyes again. I wanted it to be the moment that I *knew* the dress was the one.

I wanted to experience it so desperately that I was afraid I would try to force it. What if that moment didn't happen to me?

I gave the wonderful girl who helped us all the pictures I'd printed, and she started pulling dresses. I tried on one after another, and even though I'd envisioned them looking perfect on me, they didn't.

I knew I didn't want a strapless, beaded dress with a train. I was adamant with the sales girl. So we tried on poufy tulle dresses, sleeved dresses, A-line and ruched styles. And they were all epic fails.

Disappointed, my mom and I were getting ready to leave when the sweet salesgirl told me to wait.

"I have an idea," she said. "Let me pull a dress that I think will be perfect."

She grabbed a strapless beaded dress with a small train from the racks and brought it to my dressing room.

"Trust me," she said, smiling.

I put the dress on, and even though I wanted to keep my eyes squeezed tight and not look until I came out in front of my mom, I couldn't resist taking a peek in the fitting room mirror.

And I knew.

There is a moment when you're looking at yourself in the mirror, but instead of seeing your flaws and insecurities, you see the most beautiful woman in the world. Your fingers lightly graze the fabric and you stare, breathless, at the woman in the mirror.

I didn't have to say anything.

My mom knew too. And she purchased the expensive dress on the spot, much to my excitement and amazement. When I quietly protested about the cost, my mom grabbed my hand and looked me straight in the eye, even though I'm a few inches taller. "I saw the look in your eyes," she said. "And I knew we couldn't leave without it."

All the angst over hoping I'd have that special moment was for nothing. Because, I did experience it. It's real! It's not just something you hear about on TV or in romance novels. It happens. And it is my prayer, sweet one, that you will have that moment as well.

## Cold Feet

While your nose is buried in magazines and venue brochures, keep your eyes wide open for any red flags that pop up. People relax a little in their relationship during this time. The flurry of planning lets guards down, so be ready for anything.

What a whirlwind relationships are. While you're dating you're worried about making sure the person is awesome and wondering if he's "the one." It's couple-focused and "us" driven. Engagement can turn into a different story. It's extremely easy to get so wrapped up in the plotting, processing, planning, and preparations, that we forget to focus on our relationship.

When Justin and I got engaged, my mom sat me down. "I want you to know," she said, "that if at any point you realize you don't want to go through with the wedding, you can stop it." I smiled at her and started to object, but she rested a hand gently on my arm.

"I'm serious. Even if you are already down the aisle, I will not be mad at all about the money we spent on the wedding. The money means nothing if you think you're about to make a mistake." She chuckled. "But please figure out early if you're going to walk away."

My mom loves Justin, and I knew her words came from a serious place in her heart. She was giving me permission to leave if it wasn't right. How thankful I am for all the work Justin and I put into our dating relationship.

On my wedding day, I looked into Justin's clear green eyes and knew I was making the smartest decision of my life and the ultimate decision of my heart.

> It's that moment where you stand at a crossroads in your life and have to make a decision whether forever is the path you want to travel together.

I think Justin and I experienced "cold feet" pre-engagement with our breakup. It's that moment where you stand at a crossroads in your life and have to make a decision whether forever is the path you want to travel together. I'm thankful we experienced it at the same time and got it out of the way.

Many couples will say that one or both of them had some sort of aha! moment when they searched their soul, wondering if they were ready to make the step of marriage. It's more than a step; it's a leap. No longer are you in charge of just yourself. Now you check with someone else before you make dinner, go to the store or make plans for the weekend. You combine your money, use some of the same toiletries, and share a bed.

So it's better to warm those feet up before you're running down the aisle.

## Allison and Matthew's Story

Matthew was my boyfriend, confidant, and best friend.

Marrying him was the next logical step.

One day after class, we drove out to the lakefront. It was the first place Matthew told me he loved me, and where we occasionally did Bible studies. We were sitting on the rocks out by the water, when he proposed.

He got on his knee and put the ring on my finger. Once it hit me that this was actually happening, I got super nervous, and when I'm nervous I start rambling. I looked at him and said, "I don't know how to be a fiancée. I've been a girlfriend, I've mentally prepared to be a wife, but fiancée?"

He laughed and said, "You're a girlfriend who plans a wedding."

So plan a wedding, I did. We celebrated our engagement with family, set a date, and I started making plans. But something started to not feel right. I loved Matthew, but the seriousness of marriage hit me, and I wasn't sure if I was doing the right thing. A girlfriend of mine said it best: "He's your best friend and you'll do anything to keep that friendship, including marrying him. "

It was true.

I would've done anything to keep our friendship and not hurt him. But I *was* hurting him. Matthew is a fantastic man, and any woman would be lucky to have him. I realized that being happy wasn't enough. I would have been unsatisfied, not unhappy. He and I were always happy—we only fought maybe five times in three years—but I needed more.

So to the shock of our family and friends, I gave him back the ring. Some people say you can't be friends with your ex, but Matthew and I have shattered that lie. We see each other at church, hang out, and talk all the time, but not like we used to.

While it wasn't easy, the risk of hurting him now was minor compared to the hurt of an unfulfilled marriage. I love Matthew, but I'm not *in love* with Matthew. I know I made the right decision, and I'm thankful for the godly people in my life that supported me through it.

## Last Chance to Change

I confess, I was shocked when Allison told me she and Matthew had called off the wedding. I thought they were perfect for each other, but I was so proud of her for listening to the little voice and tug in her heart that was telling her this wasn't the path she needed to take. I know whoever Matthew and Allison end up marrying will truly be the perfect people for them, because they'll be listening a lot closer to their heads and hearts.

Ladies, listen hard and listen good: There is zero incentive for a man to change after you are married. In fact, everything that annoys you now will grate on your nerves later. Even the cute things will find a way to annoy you.

I *hate* when I can hear people chewing (*or breathing, but that's neither here nor there*). If their mouths are open while eating, forget it. My appetite vanishes.

When Justin is hungry and eating fast, the noises he makes are funny, and I always thought it was cute . . . not the noise, but just that he was so hungry that he was making noise.

Anyway, last night, *literally last night*, I was annoyed at him for no reason. In my head I tried to come up with something to blame on him for my annoyance, but he hadn't done anything. Which made me feel even more annoyed.

So we were sitting on the couch after I made amazing barbeque chicken nachos, plates in hand. I could hear him gulping down his food—the same sound that I've always thought was cute—and with each swallow I became more and more irritated. I think I scowled out loud.

Nine years of marriage have taught me that remaining silent keeps the fight brewing in my heart at bay. While I internally wrestled with my disdain, Justin finished his plate and went to the kitchen for seconds.

I prayed for God to remove my nasty attitude and, thankfully, Justin wasn't as hungry with his second portion, so I was able to eat in peace . . . *and silence.*

The cute things will annoy you later.

The bad habits will destroy you.

When we were two months away from our wedding, Justin confessed something he'd done. No, he didn't cheat, but while the specifics aren't important, let's just say I didn't know how to handle the information. I think the stress of wedding plans and other life occurrences made my reaction more explosive than he expected.

He was still on active duty with the Marines, and even though he was becoming known for his change in character, old habits die hard. The people you sin with are hard to live with if they aren't concerned with the consequences of their behavior. And one thing his buddies hadn't changed were the behaviors Justin had left behind.

I worked as a live-in nanny for a family from my church. We arrived there late at night, arguing loudly, and I was afraid the family (or neighbors) would wake up and get mad.

The only light was from a single lamppost at the end of the cul-de-sac. I stood by my car and he stood next to his. It's funny how people physically separate during arguments. Now when we fight, we force ourselves to hold hands. *Well, I force him to hold mine.*

Justin crossed his arms and leaned against the hood of his Honda. I remembered how he made me miss my birthday dinner to buy that stupid car, which added fuel to my already blazing temper. *Eleven years later, we still have that stupid car.*

As I slouched over my Saturn, my arms resting on the trunk, my head bent, I went over my options. My soul was caught in a mental versus emotional battle. My head would ask a question and my heart would answer. My heart cried out and my head responded. And in the midst of my weakness, I prayed for the Holy Spirit to groan with words I could not express (see Rom. 8:26).

What would I tell the girls in my youth group if they were in this situation?

*Don't put up with this.*

Isn't he truly sorry?

*Would he be doing this if he were?*

If I don't put an end to this situation now, will it continue?

*Most certainly.*

Am I willing to live with it?

*I'm worth more than that.*

Am I ready to walk away from our engagement? Our future? Our life?

*I don't want to.*

Resentment burned in my soul. Why should I have to deal with this? We'd recovered from our horrible breakup, and here we were again at a crossroads. If I didn't put my foot down now, I'd have no leverage later.

Ultimatums are risky, but with my future on the line, I had no choice. I threw the dice.

I lifted my head and he walked toward me. An invisible wall prevented him from coming too close. I spoke softly but firmly.

"If you don't talk to someone, I'm ending this."

Silence.

*The first person to speak loses. The first person to speak loses.* I repeated the mantra in my head, daring him to say no, praying that he'd say yes.

"Fine," he said with a flippant shrug of his shoulders.

"Tonight." My chin tilted up as I squared my shoulders, bracing for his rebuttal.

It was near midnight, after all.

"I'm not calling anybody tonight. That's ridiculous." He backed away from me with a push of his hands against the unseen wall. He started back to his car.

"I'm not kidding, *Jus-tin*," I hissed at him.

He turned on his heel and glared at me. "Who am I supposed to call, *Beth-a-ny*." He rarely ever called me by name; the iciness stung my heart.

I gave a suggestion and he scoffed. "I'm not calling him."

"Yes, you are," I said. "You tell him I'm calling off the wedding unless he talks to you right now. He's probably awake, and if not, he'll understand. You have to be accountable to someone besides me or *this won't work*." Justin was leaving the next day to go back south to his unit. This was a now-or-never situation.

I don't have a p-p-poker face, but I wasn't bluffing.[3] Each word carried a proverbial brick, and each pause slathered wet cement. Word by word, brick by brick, I built a foundation of adamancy. By him making the call immediately, I could stop construction and knock down the wall I was building while the cement was still wet.

Tomorrow was too late. I don't take sledgehammers to my heart.

I loved him too much to let his sin destroy him. Making the phone call meant he loved me enough to work on it.

He made the call.

Praise God that sin is conquerable. There were a few slip-ups, some moments of weakness, but with the help of Jesus, Justin mastered the temptation.

I am so thankful that Justin dealt with his issue. While I was angry at him for what he did, I was more angry for the position he put me in. I *knew* I would have to call off the wedding. I loved him too much to let him get away with his thorn in the flesh (see 2 Cor. 12:7). He loved me enough to conquer it.

## Windy and Justin's Story

It was New Year's Eve and we had just attended the wedding of Justin's grandmother to her longtime companion, Louis. It was such a sweet wedding. The whole family headed back to her house to have a night full of games and New Year's Eve celebration after she and her new groom had left for their honeymoon.

At some point in the evening, I headed to the guest shower to clean up and change into more comfortable clothes for the night. Justin's family is SO LOUD when they are all together. I remember getting into the shower and hearing Uncle Eddie and Aunt Rose's loud cackles as they reminisced about funny childhood stories.

Curiously, when my shower ended, the whole house was dead silent. It was so weird! I got dressed and wrapped my hair in a towel, turban-style, and peeked my head out the bathroom door. Silence.

I looked down and saw a trail of Hershey kisses leading down the hallway. So, being the chocolate-loving woman that I am, naturally I followed them. They led down the hallway into the master bedroom . . . into the master bathroom and into a large shower with a frosted glass door. I opened the door and saw TONS of roses and rose petals all over and a small card that said "Windy" on it. I stepped inside the shower to retrieve the note.

My heart began to pound as I tried to wrap my brain around what was happening. I opened the note and read:

> *Windy,*
>     *If I promise to "kiss" the ground you walk on, and "shower" you with love, will you be mine forever?*
>     *Love, Justin*

I turned around and there was Justin on one knee with a shiny diamond ring. He smiled and asked those four little words. "Will you marry me?" Of course, I shrieked, "Yes!" and we hugged in the middle of the shower. His family started cheering from the master bedroom, and I saw about 20 pairs of eyeballs staring from the dark room behind us!!

I immediately asked, "How am I going to tell my parents we were in the shower together when you proposed?!"

*(Author's Note: Justin and Windy were married August 2, 2003, and they have two beautiful children.)*

## Mallory and David's Story

David and I took a trip with my family to Las Vegas for a week. I didn't even think about David proposing, nor did

I know that he bought a ring three months earlier! We spent Sunday and Monday sightseeing, and David kept saying how much he wanted to go see Paris and the Eiffel Tower.

On Tuesday, we bought our tickets for a show that night. David kept holding my arm instead of my hand, and he later told me it was because his hands wouldn't stop shaking, so he had to keep them in his pockets!

Anyway, we went to the show and David ended up winning $50 before we went in. He said "I can put this toward your ring." Sneaky.

When we arrived at the Eiffel Tower, my mom said she didn't want to go up because she is deathly afraid of heights; they would wait for us at the bottom. David invited my brother and his girlfriend in hopes to throw me off that something special was going to happen. It worked, because I had no idea.

We got to the entrance of the tower and had our picture taken. I tried to stand on David's left side for the picture, but he made me switch to his right because "it was his better side." Little did I know that he didn't want me to feel the RING that he had in his coat pocket.

We got in the elevator and began the 462-foot climb. Once we got to the top, I started taking pictures and walking around, but David kept trying to get me to come around to the other side of the tower. When he finally got me in position, the Bellagio fountains below us went off and the entire Strip looked BEAUTIFUL.

My brother's girlfriend said she wanted a picture of us, so David and I got together and posed. After she took it, David said, "Wait, I want to take one more," spun around and got on one knee. I immediately started freaking out and crying. He pulled out the beautiful ring and said in front of everyone "Mallory, will you marry me?"

Of course, I screamed, "YES!" and he spun me around. We kissed and hugged and I told perfect strangers that we were getting married and showed my ring to anyone who would look.

It was almost ten o'clock Vegas-time which meant that it was 1:00 a.m. at home. I called my best friend, who had known it was going to happen for three months (you guys are so sneaky!) and celebrated with her. We then called family and woke up everyone to tell them the news.

When we got back to the bottom where my parents were waiting, my mom immediately started to cry, and we hugged and jumped around. We went to a cute little restaurant inside the Paris hotel to celebrate. Of course, I had to visit the gift shop and buy all the little Eiffel Tower trinkets I could find.

I was taken by total surprise and am so grateful to my amazing friends and family for making this so special. I have the most amazing fiancé and can't wait to marry him! Vegas will always have a piece of my heart now!

*(Author's note: David and Mallory were married on May 14, 2011.)*

## Our Story

When Justin was on his active duty assignment, we would talk every night after the sun went down. I would go outside and stand in my driveway, and pray for clear skies. As soon as we found the Orion constellation, we'd say, "I love you," and stare at the stars, knowing the love of our life was looking at the same sky. *The characters in the movie* Dear John *would look at the moon, but I was excited to know that Justin and I had our Orion thing first.*

He actually proposed twice. The first time, the time I count, was a slip on his part, I think. He'd been offered a more permanent position in West Palm, but he didn't want to take it without talking to me first. He told me about the offer, and then said, "If I ask you to marry me, what would you say?" He didn't mean it as his proposal, just that if I wasn't planning on marriage so soon after our breakup, he was going to decline the job.

I did what any girlfriend would do. I made him squirm.

"Are you asking me?" I said, waiting with bated breath. I was totally caught off guard and hadn't thought about him making the military a more permanent career choice, but I would have followed him to the ends of the earth.

He awkwardly explained the reasoning behind his question as he realized he should have worded that a little differently. "Well, I want to talk to your father, and I didn't know how you felt . . . I didn't want to drive all the way up there and not see you . . . you'd find out . . ."

I felt bad for making him uncomfortable. He was too sweet to be toyed with, so I interrupted him. "Yes," I said. "If you ask me to marry you, I will say yes."

I didn't tell anybody except my grandma about our conversation. He obviously was upset with himself for showing his hand, and it wouldn't be fun to share the news that we were "almost engaged" without a ring. My grandma was thrilled that we'd reconciled, and she gave me her blessing.

For the time that Justin counts, I was staying at his parents' house so we could attend our friends' wedding. Justin, a parachute rigger, planned to have me come to the drop zone where he was scheduled to jump. He wanted to have each of the jumpers before him to each hold a sign spelling out "Will You Marry Me," with him as the final jumper with the ring. The jump was canceled.

On December 6, 2003, we left our friends dancing the night away at their beautiful wedding reception. We pulled into the empty lot across from his parents' house, and he asked me to help him carry in some of the Toys 4 Tots donations he'd collected. I walked around the driver's side and waited for him to open the trunk. I saw a mound of toys and leaned in for a closer inspection. Then I heard Justin say my name.

I looked over to find him down on one knee. *He told me later he could see Orion behind me as he looked up at my face.* "Bethany," he said, as I clapped my hands over my mouth in surprise, "will you marry me?" He opened a ring box and inside was the perfect multi-princess cut diamond ring.

I started to cry, because that's what I do, nodded my head and said, "Yes, yes, of course. Stand up!" He rose, put the ring on my finger and kissed me under Orion's approving glow. Then we went inside, showed his family, and went outside to recreate it and get pictures taken. *Get pictures taken!*

## Not Destined for Failure

We filled out the paperwork for our marriage license, and while we were waiting for the clerk to call our name, we watched an older couple walk out of a side set of double doors. I say older, but they were probably in their late thirties. *Amazing how perception changes the older you get!* The Justice of the Peace had married them, and they were holding hands and smiling.

After the clerk finally called us up to swear us in and make our license official, we smiled at each other. She gave us our packet without smiling, and we were on our way.

When we got to the car, Justin reached inside the bag and laughed at what was inside. He pulled out a booklet titled *How to Get a Divorce in Florida* or something like that. Thanks, legal system. No wonder so many marriages end in divorce—they give you a how-to guide before you even say your vows. Talk about setting yourself up for failure! That's kind of like telling a kid not to have sex, and then passing out the condoms.

We threw the entire packet away.

* * * * * * * * *

"May the Lord deal with me, be it ever so severely, if anything but death separates you and me" (Ruth 1:17).

* * * * * * * * *

"Divorce" is a dirty word for us, and it's not an option. We don't think divorce. We don't threaten divorce. We may think, *I don't want to be near you right now,* but not *I don't want to be near you ever again.* We promised to be together for better or for worse; in fact, we took it a step further and included in our vows, "May the

LORD deal with me, be it ever so severely, if anything but death separates you and me."[4]

Even now, as I sit next to my sexy man sleeping in the recliner next to me (bless his tired heart), I L.O.V.E. that Justin's out here with me in our back family room because he'd rather fall asleep on the couch than go to bed without me. I hope that never changes.

I've enjoyed this journey with you, my new friend. I hope you tuck this book into a safe place and refer to it as you enter each new dating phase. If you are still waiting for Prince Charming, his horse might be lame, or perhaps he hasn't asked God for directions yet. Stay rooted in Christ so that He knows where to lead your man.

You are God's crown of creation, special and precious. Never settle for a man who doesn't recognize your worth. When you're ready to say "I do" to the godly man who has pursued you, I wish you a beautiful wedding and an incredible life together.

You know, the rules don't stop with dating. There are tested principles—certain standards that ensure a beautiful, long marriage. We've found that other happily married couples have many of the same "house rules" that we do, and some have an interesting system to keep their marriage love affair-resistant, rock-solid and divorce-proof.

Your husband should continue his pursuit of you in your marriage.

I can't wait to show you how, but that's another story.

**Notes**

1. Gary D. Chapman, *The Five Love Languages: The Secret to Love That Lasts* (Chicago, IL: Northfield Publishing, 2010).
2. Reliant K, "Pressing On" (Nashville, TN: Gotee Records, 2001).
3. Lady Gaga, "Poker Face" (New York: Sony/ATV Music Publishing, 2008). That was for you, Tara.
4. Ruth's vow to her mother-in-law, Naomi. See Ruth 1:16-17.

# Study Guide

## Chapter 1: Confidence

1. Name three of your strengths.
2. What was your dream as a little girl?
3. Is there a career or goal that combines your strengths and dreams? What is it?
4. To what areas of your life do you dedicate the most time?
5. On page 15, I state, "Self-esteem should be called God-esteem." Do you agree? Why, or why not?
6. Have you ever been in a situation where you got worse service or better service based on how you were dressed? Explain.
7. Have you ever been intimidated by a prettier woman? What causes women to size each other up?
8. List the people in your life from whom you need reassurance or approval. Why is it so important to you to make them happy?
9. What are some reasons God might make us wait to meet our Prince Charming?
10. What are some specific ways that you can make yourself feel more confident?

## Chapter 2: Preparation

1. How did the poem referred to at the beginning of the chapter make you feel? Do you agree with my reaction?
2. Should we marry our best friend?
3. Do you want to be "friends first" with your future husband, or are you dreaming of an "attraction at first sight"?
4. What's the importance of keeping girlfriends while dating? Why is it a mistake to alienate yourself from your friends?
5. How important is it to you to marry a virgin? Is this a deal breaker for you?

6. Have you prepared your heart for the amount of sexual experience your guy might have had? Does his sexual past become a deal breaker? Do you want to be equally matched experience-wise?

7. Have you ever regretted confiding in someone? Why is it important to let the guy share his past first? Do you have to tell him when he tells you? When is it "too late" to share?

8. In this chapter, I state that it was no coincidence that my prayers coincided with my husband's worst spiritual period. Does that make you want to start praying now for your future husband? Does God help our future spouse when we pray?

9. Which accomplishments listed from *Pride and Prejudice* do you wish you knew how to do? Which ones can you do? What other talents do you have?

10. Which Disney princess do you relate to most? Why? Which one do you want to be when Prince Charming finds you?

## Chapter 3: Qualifying

1. In what ways did Justin's flaws only add to his "perfection"? How can someone's faults add to his desirability?

2. What are your top five qualifications for a husband?

3. What is on your shallow list? Come on . . . share!

4. Be honest—where does "Christian" fall on your list? What is your definition of a "Christian"?

5. Why does Jesus say not to date/marry a non-Christian?

6. What are some challenges for couples when one person is a Christian and the other person is not?

7. What areas of theology are important for you and your future spouse to agree on?

8. Did you ever want to be any of the television characters that I listed in this chapter? If so, what actresses do you find yourself imitating?

9. Do you agree with the words, "If you fall in love, you can fall out of love" (see page 47)? Explain.

10. Do you think it's better to "grow in love"? Why or why not?

# Chapter 4: Positioning

1. What does chasing a guy look like?
2. What does a guy chasing you look like?
3. What is negative attention? Is it better to receive no attention than to receive negative attention? Why?
4. Has a guy chased you before? Was he cute or creepy? Share how it made you feel. Did he catch you?
5. What are you supposed to do when a guy you like starts pursuing you? What if it's a guy you don't like?
6. In this chapter I mention that females can spot insecurity with the snap of a finger. What are some ways we demonstrate insecurity?
7. What do we do if the guy we like doesn't pursue us?
8. Name some ways to be mysterious without acting like a weirdo.
9. Is a relationship easier to *start* long-distance or *continue* long-distance? What are some ways to ensure you can learn about someone you've met online?
10. In what ways can long-distance relationships be taxing on a couple? What can couples do to make the distance between them seem shorter?

# Chapter 5: Attire

1. What did you like about Phil Chalmers's illustration in this chapter on advertising?
2. What was your favorite modesty tip? Which tip is the hardest for you to follow?
3. When you read about the "palm rule," did you check your shirt? Are you going to start using this as a basis for your tops? Why or why not? What can using the "palm rule" avoid when it comes to guys that are taller than us?
4. Have you ever been in a situation where you felt uncomfortable based on what you were wearing? Explain.
5. Have you ever considered that our outfits can lead men to lust? To masturbate? How much of the responsibility lies on our shoulders?

6. What is the correct balance between God's definition of beauty in 1 Peter 3:3-4 and the world's standard? Can we achieve both?
7. Do you find yourself dressing more modestly for church than you do for school, work or a social engagement?
8. What are your criteria for a cute outfit? For a modest outfit? Are they the same? Explain.
9. Why are first impressions important?
10. What are some ways to ensure a great first impression?

## Chapter 6: Femininity

1. What's the difference between being a tomboy and not being girly? Are the two mutually exclusive?
2. How do you make yourself more feminine?
3. Do you see "being girly" as a negative? Why or why not?
4. What is the stigma with being girly?
5. In this chapter I state that femininity is internal. What if you don't feel feminine? What can you do?
6. What's the difference between low, mid- and high-maintenance? Where do you fall?
7. Do you consider yourself to be gentle? Would others consider you to be gentle? Does God?
8. How can we demonstrate gentleness to others?
9. What are some benefits of having a mentor?
10. I said that there is strength in gentleness. Do you agree? Who do you know who exhibits this amazing character trait? What are some ways you can demonstrate strength in gentleness?

## Chapter 7: Availability

1. Has a guy ever worked hard to get your attention? What would you do if someone created an ice-shaped heart with a note in it just to ask you out?
2. What are your thoughts on the Wednesday Rule? When is it okay to break it?

3. Why should you be the first one to leave?
4. Why shouldn't girls ask for the second date? What can't you be sure of a guy's motivation for agreeing to a second date if you are the one who sets it up?
5. With social media at our fingertips, why shouldn't girls contact a guy first?
6. Why shouldn't girls practice submitting to their boyfriends? Is dating the time to practice for marriage? Why or why not?
7. Why doesn't your boyfriend deserve exclusive amounts of your time?
8. Can breakups be a good thing for a relationship? Explain. Has this happened to you?
9. How do you keep a breakup from turning into a manipulation tool?
10. Why is it important to keep your friendships with other people intact while you're dating?

## Chapter 8: Communication

1. How frustrating is it when a guy you like isn't as mature as you want him to be?
2. Have you ever been the victim of gossip? False gossip? Have you been the spreader of gossip?
3. Allison's reputation was on the line when she was accused of a one-night stand that never happened. How can a girl repair her reputation? How do you feel about the double standard?
4. Are you a flirt? Is a "boy fast" something you should consider doing? Is there another way to control or monitor flirting?
5. It sounds nice when people say they pray about dating someone. Aren't the words "I have to pray about it" used as a way to get out of doing something? Have you ever prayed for God's peace before getting into a relationship? Do you wish you had?
6. Why should a guy say "I love you" first?
7. How can you show appreciation to your boyfriend without going overboard?

8.  Why is it okay for guys to share their past before girls share? When should you share your history?

9.  What texts or photos would you delete off your phone before handing it to your parents, a church leader or mentor?

10. Have you ever sexted? How did it make you feel? Do you regret sending the messages or photos? Why do we get caught up in it?

## Chapter 9: Boundaries

1.  Where do you place your boundary in a dating relationship?

2.  Do you agree that the people in the relationship need to discuss boundaries? What happens if one person's boundary goes further than the other person's? Who moves? Does it depend on which boundary it is?

3.  Would your parents move your boundary backward if they could? Would they move it forward?

4.  Why do we feel guilty when we cross our boundaries?

5.  When is it appropriate to move a boundary forward? (For example, from holding hands to put arms round; or hold close and kiss to further physical contact)

6.  Why is it hard to move a boundary back once it's been crossed?

7.  Where do you think God would set your boundary?

8.  Describe a time when you're thankful you stuck to your boundary.

9.  I know this is personal, but when was a time when you regretted crossing a boundary?

10. We know that God forgives us when we mess up, but do you look at yourself and truly believe that God forgives? Why or why not?

## Chapter 10: Kissing

1.  What did your "first kiss fantasy" look like? Was your first kiss everything you dreamed it would be? If not, what would you change?

2. How long did you wait before experiencing your first kiss?

3. If you haven't kissed anyone, are you proud that you've waited? How long are you going to continue to wait? Do you think you place a higher value on your kisses than if you had kissed someone already?

4. Do you agree that the boy should initiate the kiss? Why or why not?

5. What are your feelings about hickeys? How do you feel when you see someone walking around with one?

6. How long can you kiss someone before you've been kissing "too long"?

7. Have you ever thought about the fact that you might be kissing someone else's future spouse? Does that bother you? Explain.

8. What is your opinion on French kissing? Is it appropriate for a first kiss?

9. If the person is a bad kisser, do you let him know? How?

10. Have you ever practiced kissing on your arm? The back of your hand? Pillow? Something else?

## Chapter 11: Kissing Plus

1. What is the definition of Further Physical Contact (FPC)? Does your definition match mine? Does your definition match your boyfriend's?

2. Does FPC fall within the Bible's "sexual immorality" limits? Why or why not?

3. Verbalize three or four "activities" that fall in this category. Which ones are acceptable in today's society as "standard" for a dating relationship? Does God think they are acceptable? How about your parents? Explain any discrepancies.

4. Do you think most girls participate in FPC out of guilt, boredom or fear of losing a guy? Why do you think that girls initiate it?

5. Should a future spouse be told about prior FPC experience? When?

6. Should people who participate in FPC get tested for STDs? Why do you think the majority of people do not?

7. What do you consider the furthest activity of FPC before sliding into the Have Sex category?

8. Have you been trapped in a Sin > Repent > Sin > Repent cycle? Did you feel like God would stop listening to you? How did you release yourself from that cycle?

9. In this chapter, I stated that I often fooled around when I didn't want to do so. How can sin feel good and not feel good at the same time?

10. Why does fooling around with a boyfriend make it easier to fool around with the next one?

## Chapter 12: Sex

1. Besides the fact that God said to wait, what are some other reasons to wait until marriage to have sex?

2. Do you think having sex on the first or second date is as common as it appears on television?

3. Our culture rarely shows "hot" married people having sex. Why do we as a society glorify premarital sex, but downplay married sex?

4. Are there any stereotypes about sex that I mentioned in this chapter that you thought were true? Were there any that I didn't mention?

5. What are your thoughts on Mack's conversation with Justin?

6. What are your thoughts about Ben and Amy's story?

7. What does it mean when the author says "sex binds"?

8. Why am I not scared of my husband cheating? Is there a connection between abstinence and fidelity? Explain.

9. What are some of the lies we tell ourselves? Which ones do you believe? Why are they lies?

10. Have you ever thought about the emotional pain of dealing with your spouse's past? Why did the women Justin slept with hurt my heart so deeply? How do think you'll feel if your future husband has a similar past?

## Chapter 13: Exit Strategy

1. What are some of your deal breakers?
2. Why do you have to uphold your end of the deal if your guy crosses the line?
3. What does dating with "eyes wide open" mean?
4. How do you think with your heart and love with your head?
5. What's the problem with on-again, off-again relationships?
6. Which breakup reason is the worst? Do any of them seem silly or trivial? Are you willing to adopt them as deal breakers?
7. What are the levels of "knowing" in love? Where are you at in your relationship? Do you think most people believe they are in a "higher level of knowing" than they really are? Why do think that is?
8. Do you think I did the right thing by calling Justin the next morning to confess that I'd kissed Evan? Would it have been a big deal if I had kept it to myself?
9. Why do we have to be careful about who we trust in regard to our relationships?
10. Did Evan take advantage of the situation, or was he an innocent bystander? Was Justin right to be angry at both of us? Explain.

## Chapter 14: Engagement

1. How much say-so should the groom have in planning the wedding? Is it realistic to expect him to be as involved as the bride?
2. Should the bride or the person paying for the wedding have the final say in regard to venue, flowers, reception, photographer and so on?
3. When should a couple move in together? Do they really need to wait until after the wedding?
4. Why do you still have to keep your "eyes open" during engagement?
5. Would you be willing to call off a wedding if your fiancé pulled a deal breaker?

6.  In an earlier chapter, I stated that breakups are not to be used as manipulation tools. Was I manipulating Justin with my ultimatum? If so, what should I have done instead? If not, what is the difference?

7.  Why is it important to be selfish about your wedding?

8.  Do you believe in the "aha!" moment when you try on the perfect dress? Why or why not?

9.  Do you believe in "cold feet"? Explain.

10. Which engagement story is your favorite? How do you want your fiancé to propose?

*You can connect with Bethany at www.BethanyJett.com.*
*She's eager to hear from you!*

# Also Available from Regal

**Eyes Wide Open**
Brienne Murk (of Myrrh)
ISBN 978-0-8307-4492-3
ISBN 0-8307-4492-4

You've heard the abstinence message. You aren't sleeping together. You didn't even kiss. So why do you feel so guilty? God cares how you treat your feelings just as much as how you treat your body—and He has a plan to keep you on the right track. In *Eyes Wide Open*, author Brienne Murk describes the necessity of guarding your most precious treasure: your heart. As a single young woman, she dealt with the same relational issues that face every young person, and she candidly shares her experiences and her mistakes. With *Eyes Wide Open*, you will learn how easy it is to let your emotions get the best of you—but, even more importantly, how to protect yourself from heartbreak. Whether you are in a relationship, just got out of one, are hoping for one to start or just have friends of the opposite sex, this book will equip you to have healthy relationships in all aspects of your life.